American Government in Action

Political Parties of the United States

Michael Kronenwetter

Enslow Publishers, Inc.

40 Industrial Road   PO Box 38
Box 398   Aldershot
Berkeley Heights, NJ 07922 Hants GU12 6BP
USA   UK

http://www.enslow.com

Library of Congress Cataloging-in-Publication Data

Kronenwetter, Michael.
     Political parties of the United States / Michael Kronenwetter.
        p. cm. — (American government in action)
     Includes bibliographical references and index.
     Summary: Discusses the history, workings, importance, and powers
of political parties in the United States.
     ISBN 0-89490-537-6
     1. Political parties—United States—Juvenile literature. [1. Political
parties.] I. Title. II. Series.
JK2261.K76 1996
324.273'09—dc20   95-15928
                                              CIP
                                               AC

Printed in the United States of America

10 9 8 7 6 5 4

Illustration Credits:
Illinois State Historical Library, pp. 43, 97; Kansas State Historical
Society, pp. 112, 114; Library of Congress, pp. 17, 21, 30, 36, 39, 47,
64, 69; State Historical Society of Wisconsin, pp. 41, 52.

Cover Illustrations:
AP/Wide World Photos

Contents

Hail, Hail, The Gang's All Here!

July 13–16, 1992.

The scene is Madison Square Garden, New York City. The occasion is the 1992 national convention of the Democratic party of the United States. It could be the national convention of either major party in any recent year; they all look and feel and sound very much alike.

The massive hall is decorated in red, white, and blue. It is packed with people. Some sit quietly on the thousands of folding chairs lined up in rows across the huge room. Others move about the hall, stopping now and then to talk earnestly to someone. Still others are dancing in the aisles, singing along as the band strikes up the catchy old political anthem, "Hail, Hail, the Gang's All Here."

The gang *is* all here! These are the delegates of the party, chosen by party members and voters all over the country to come together to do the party's business.

They gather like this once every four years, flocking from every corner of the United States—from Florida to Alaska, and from Hawaii to Maine, and from the United States territories, like Guam and the Virgin Islands, as well.

The delegates have come for many reasons. This event is, among other more important things, a big party. Many are here to enjoy the experience, to renew old friendships, and to make new ones. They have other serious things to do as well. They need to discuss what has happened in the four years since the last convention, and to plan the party's strategy for the next four years. While they are here, they will debate about what the party should stand for, and argue about controversial issues like cutting back on defense programs, reforming welfare, and raising rich people's taxes. In the process, they will write a platform that will explain the party's views to the people of the United States.

Most important of all, they are here to nominate a candidate for President of the United States, and to launch the election campaign that they hope will sweep their choice into the White House.

Picking presidential candidates is what political parties are best known for. Some people think it is what they do best. Every President except George Washington has been nominated by a political party.

Every President since Franklin Pierce, who took office in 1852, has belonged to one of only two major parties—either the Republicans or the Democrats.

Presidential candidates are formally named by a vote of the delegates on the second to last day of each presidential convention. Still, everybody knows that this convention is going to nominate Governor Bill Clinton of Arkansas. He already had more delegates' votes pledged to him than he needed before the convention even began.

In the meantime, before the nomination, there is business to be done—and there is a show to be put on!

Political conventions are televised. Knowing this, the parties try to present themselves in the best possible light to the millions of viewers watching across the country.

Most national conventions have one keynote speaker whose job is to give a stirring speech that gets things off to a good start. This convention goes further. It has three keynote speakers—Senator Bill Bradley of New Jersey, Governor Zell Miller of Georgia, and Barbara Jordan of Texas. They do their jobs well, rallying the party faithful by attacking the Republicans, and praising Bill Clinton as a candidate who understands the American people.

The theme of their speeches, and of the whole Democratic convention, is change. A Republican, George Bush, is President, and this convention hopes to change that by starting a Democrat down the road to the White House.

The year 1992 has been proclaimed the "Year of the Woman," so the party takes the opportunity to showcase women in key roles at the convention. The chairperson is Governor Ann Richards of Texas. She makes sure that six women candidates running for the Senate have a chance to speak on the very first night, when lots of people are sure to be watching on television.

Over the next two days, there are many moving and exciting moments. The delegates debate the platform issues and vote on them. Two of the party's best-loved figures inspire the delegates with their speeches: The activist leader Jesse Jackson cheers the party's liberals with a stirring reminder of the Democrats' traditional liberal values. Governor Mario Cuomo of New York inspires the entire convention with a nominating speech that celebrates Bill Clinton as the "Comeback Kid" and promises that he will be elected President in November.

Finally the second to last night of the convention has come, and it is time to vote. All the delegates gather on the floor, each under a big sign with their state's or territory's name on it. A long roll call of the states is held, with each delegation voting in turn. The bigger states have more delegates, and get more votes than the smaller states or the territories, because they have more people.

The roll call continues until Clinton's vote total tops the number he needs to win the nomination. The hall explodes with cheers. Thousands of balloons drop from the ceiling, and a massive celebration begins. The band strikes up. Chants of "We want Bill" fill the hall.

Before long, the delegates get their wish; Bill Clinton himself arrives. Now the delegates really go wild, waving their hands, cheering, and jumping up and down in enthusiasm. Clinton thanks the delegates, and leaves to more cheers.

The next night, Clinton formally accepts the nomination. He speaks, he says, for "all the people who do the work, pay the taxes,. . . and play by the rules . . . our forgotten middle class."[1] The band strikes up the rousing song that becomes the Clinton theme song, "Don't Stop Thinking About Tomorrow."

Clinton and his vice presidential nominee Al Gore are joined on the stage by their wives, and the two couples begin to dance to the rock tune. Delegates on the floor start dancing as well. Some delegates even begin to sing, urging each other, in the words of the song, to "think about tomorrow! Yesterday's gone. Yesterday's gone." The message going out over television is clear. This is a new, young generation of political leaders. Things have changed! It is time for a change in Washington, too: a new President.

Before long, the whole hall is rocking with music and optimism. The convention has achieved its purpose. It has become a party in every sense. It has brought Democrats together, both those in the hall and those watching across the country, in the effort to elect a President.

A month from now, the Republican party will

meet in Houston for its own convention. Its delegates will unite behind the current Republican President, George Bush, and they will renominate him for a second term. These two men—Clinton and Bush—will do battle in the presidential election of 1992. No matter how many other candidates there are, one of these two men almost certainly will win.

Although anyone can run for President, only someone nominated by one of the two main political parties has a realistic chance of becoming President of the United States.

Why should that be?

What are these political parties?

How do they work?

And why are they so powerful that they get to pick our Presidents for us?

Joining Forces

Politics, according to the *Oxford English Dictionary*, is "the science and art of government."[1] In a democratic system like ours, it includes not only the acts of people in office, but the efforts of people to win office as well.

Politics involves conflict. In any form of government, there are bound to be disagreements over issues, about what the government should do, and how things should be done. Some people will be on one side of an issue, some on the other. In a democratic system, like ours, those who find themselves together on a particular side need to work together to promote their joint interests. In essence, they become what is known as an interest group. Working together, they try to persuade more and more people to join them in asking the government to take action. They vote for, and work for, political candidates who agree with them, and oppose those who do not.

When the same people find themselves on the same sides of several different issues, they begin to work together even more extensively. They form a kind of partnership with people in other interest groups. In order to increase their influence, they support each other, even on issues that not all of them are particularly interested in. Eventually, they organize to pool their resources and make even more of an impact on government affairs.

In other words, they become a political party.

Parties, then, are political organizations that people with similar interests or opinions use to work together to accomplish their goals.

▶ The Need for Political Parties

Every modern country that claims to be democratic has at least one political party. Those that truly are democratic have more than one. It is probably impossible for a large and diverse democracy to operate without them, because people in a democracy need to work together to affect the government that controls so much of their lives. The political party gives them a way to do that.

There are many hotly conflicting views and interests in any democracy. Some of those conflicting interests are economic. Employers, for example, need to keep down the costs of running their businesses. At the same time, the people who work for them need good pay in order to support themselves and their families. One group wants to keep wages as low as possible; the other wants to raise them.

Some conflicting interests are social. Many Americans, for example, believe that violence and pornography in the media are leading to a disastrous breakdown in family values. At the same time, most creative people believe that they should be allowed to express themselves in any way they choose.

Still other conflicting interests are purely political. Liberals and conservatives, for example, have opposing philosophies of government. They have different ideas about what the government should and should not do.

Both know that the government plays a major role in the economic affairs of citizens, but liberals welcome that role, while conservatives reject it. Liberals believe that the government should actively provide economic security for individuals. Conservatives want government to keep out of people's economic lives as much as possible.

How could one politician, or one political organization, fairly represent all these conflicting views and interests? This would be impossible, yet people need their views and interests represented in government. They need some way to see to it that candidates who represent them are elected to office. Parties are the vehicles they use to find and elect those candidates.

There are two major parties in the United States today—the Democrats and the Republicans—as well as many smaller ones. The older party, the Democratic party, traces its roots back to the earliest days of constitutional government in the United States. The second major party, the Republican party, was born in the struggle over slavery before the Civil War.

▶ What Parties Do

Political parties perform many useful functions:

They provide a way for ordinary citizens to influence, and to take part in, the political process.

Parties pick candidates for office, on both the local and national levels, and help the candidates to present their ideas and principles to the public.

Once their candidates are elected, the parties give them vital support. They provide their representatives with a ready-made pool of people, energy, and ideas that help them to govern.

Finally, they help people to reach compromises about their small differences in order to work together to accomplish more important goals.

The Birth of
Political Parties

The Constitution of the United States is the blueprint for the United States political system, yet the Constitution does not mention political parties at all. This might seem odd, considering the vital role parties play in our government.

▶ The Danger of Factions

America was not supposed to have political parties—at least, that was the hope of many of the nation's founders. They dreamed of building a democratic republic, where people would be concerned with the good of the entire society, not just with themselves. They feared that if any one faction won control of the government, it would pass laws to help only its own members, regardless of the effects of these laws on everyone else.

George Washington, for example, hated the very idea of parties. He distrusted what he called "factions," groups that were primarily worried about their own interests. He despised anything that "put in the place of the delegated will of the nation the will of a party."[1]

Washington denounced "all combinations and associations . . . [designed] . . . to direct, control, counteract, or awe the regular deliberation and action" of the government. Such factions, he declared in his farewell address, would be "destructive" to the nation.[2]

Washington believed that what was good for the country was good for all the people. Sound government policies would benefit the East, the West, the North, and the South alike. People who favored political parties did not see it that way. Parties, Washington thought, were based on the divisions among Americans, not on their unity. They would divide the country; they would not bring it together. Ultimately, Washington knew, party members would come to desire their own party's power more than anything else.

Washington was particularly worried that parties would organize along geographical lines. He feared that the plantation South would set the government against the small farms and cities of the North, or that the settled East would use the government to take advantage of the frontier West.

Washington's fear that geographical factions would be destructive was soon justified. By the time

The only President who was not a member of a political party, George Washington (center) despised what he called "factions."

of the Civil War, the South and the North came to see their interests as being so opposed to each other that they could no longer cooperate for the national good. Southern Democrats insisted that the North was trampling on their region's rights, while the abolitionist wing of the Republican party felt bound to oppose the southern institution of slavery. When the South went so far as to secede from the United States altogether, the Republicans set out to preserve the Union. The Civil War was the horrible result.

The Civil War may have made some people think that Washington was right, that it would have been better if the United States had avoided division into parties altogether. It was not the parties that led to the war, though, but the economic and social differences that existed between the North and South at that time. The Democratic and Republican parties only represented those differences. They did not cause them.

▶ The Federalists

Despite the fears of many of the nation's founders, the division of American political life into two main factions began before the ink was dry on the Constitution. The revolutionaries who threw out the colonial government imposed on them by England had to decide what kind of government to put in its place—or, more accurately, what kind of governments, because the new nation would be a federation. It would be a combination of regional, or state, governments. These governments would decide on laws and policies for the individual states. The new nation would need some kind of national government as well. Some overall, central government would have to make decisions for the federation as a whole.

What kind of federal government would be best? What should its duties be? What powers should it have? These were the great questions that divided the nation's founders. One group, which came to be known as the Federalists, wanted a relatively strong central government.

These Federalists formed the first real political party in the United States. Its members were mostly well-off northerners. They were merchants, manufacturers, financiers, and owners of large plantations. They were as conservative as a group of former revolutionaries could possibly be. They distrusted the ordinary Americans who made up most of the population, and looked to aristocratic men like John Adams and Alexander Hamilton to lead them.

The Federalists controlled the government in the first years of the American republic. Although George Washington refused to join any faction, he agreed with the Federalists on most matters, and the Federalists supported him while he was in office. When he left, the self-proclaimed Federalist John Adams was elected to succeed him, and Federalists had majorities in both the House and the Senate.

Altogether, the Federalists controlled the government for a full twelve years. During that time, they worked to build a national government that would safeguard their property and protect their businesses from foreign competition. Among other things, they wanted the federal government to establish a national bank and to mint a national currency. (At this time, each state chartered its own banks, which issued each state's own legal money.) A national bank would make it much easier for people to buy and sell goods all over the young country. They considered the Constitution a loose document that gave them a lot of leeway in deciding what the federal government could do to protect American business and to promote American trade.

▶ The Democratic-Republicans

Americans who disagreed with the Federalists on key issues needed some way to unite to oppose them. They found that way in the organization that later would become the Democratic party. Ironically, the founders of the Democratic party were originally known as the Republicans, a name that would later be taken by the party that would eventually become the Democrats' greatest rival. Looking to James Madison and Thomas Jefferson for leadership, they were also called the Jeffersonian Republicans, or sometimes the Democratic-Republicans. It was not until 1828 that they officially began to call themselves, simply, the Democratic party.

The early Democrats-to-be were mostly farmers and small planters, workers, and artisans who came from the South and the frontier. They took the Constitution—and particularly the first ten amendments, the Bill of Rights—much more literally than did the Federalists. They looked to the Constitution

Thomas Jefferson was the author of the Declaration of Independence and chief founder of what would become the Democratic party.

and to the state governments to protect them from the power of the federal government.

They distrusted the wealthy eastern aristocrats whom the Federalists wanted to run the new government. They hoped for a more robust democracy, in which all educated men could vote and participate in government. (It would be more than a century before any major party would support giving the vote to women.) The Democratic-Republicans opposed all sorts of things that the Federalists stood for, including a national bank that would make it harder for small farmers and businessmen to borrow money, and tariffs that would make foreign goods harder for ordinary citizens to buy.

The different ways the two parties saw the world were shown in the different ways they reacted to the French Revolution (1789–1799). Jefferson and many others in his party sympathized with the masses who rose up and overthrew the French monarchy. They believed that the French people's revolution against their king was similar to the American colonists' early revolution against the English monarch.

The more conservative Federalists were appalled by the violence in France. In their view, the American Revolution had been carried out by men of property and good sense. The French Revolution, on the other hand, was being carried out by a crazed, bloodthirsty mob. The military battles of the American Revolution had been nothing like the mass executions of the French Reign of Terror, in which hundreds of French aristocrats, and others, were being ruthlessly beheaded in the public squares.

The fact that Jefferson's party approved of what was going on in France made the Federalists shudder. If the Republicans came to power in the United States, would they launch a Reign of Terror here? The Federalists, after all, were the gentry of America. They were the closest thing the United States had to the French aristocracy. Many American Federalists stroked their own necks fearfully when they heard about the French guillotine, and they considered the possibility that the Republicans might take over the United States government one day.

For their part, the Jeffersonians complained that the Federalists were much too cozy with the English. The Federalist government made the United States a virtual partner in the war that England and other European countries launched against revolutionary France. The Federalists not only broke off trade with France, they even ordered the United States Navy to capture French ships on the high seas. Had the colonies fought a war to free themselves from Great Britain only to do its bidding anyway?

▶ Trying to Outlaw Opposition

Arguments between the two factions got so heated that in 1798 the Federalists actually passed laws to shut the Jeffersonians up, if not to destroy them altogether. Known as the Alien and Sedition Acts, these laws make it a federal crime to make "scandalous" or "malicious" statements against the government and its policies, that is, to criticize the Federalists.

In effect, the Federalists were trying to outlaw the rival political party, or at least to forbid any vigorous opposition to the Federalists' authority that it might launch. There was a danger, if they succeeded, that the young country might become a one-party state.

The Acts were a powerful assault on the political liberties of the Jeffersonians. Several newspaper editors and Republican Congressman Matthew Lyon were sent to prison for violating them.

The new laws backfired on the Federalists. Those Americans who treasured the freedoms promised in the Bill of Rights resented the Acts and supported the Republicans. In the next election, they threw out the Federalist President, John Adams, and elected Thomas Jefferson in his place. Jefferson promptly released the jailed Republicans.

This was a key moment for American democracy and for the future of political parties. One party had set out to outlaw another. Now that the intended victim was in power, would it do the same to its opponent? It would not. Instead of turning the Alien and Sedition Acts on their opponents, the victorious Democratic-Republicans simply ignored the Acts altogether.

That established a vital precedent, a model for the major political parties in the future. They would fight bitterly with each other for control of the government, but there were limits to what they would do to each other. They would accept each other's existence, recognizing that different people had different interests in a democracy, and that they needed organizations to promote and defend those interests.

The Democrats in Power

The Federalists had ruled the country for its first decade and more. The Federalists were elitists; they were led by wealthy and well-educated men. (Only men were allowed to participate openly in politics in those days.) The Federalists saw the young country through wealthy men's eyes. They were not typical of Americans of that time, any more than the aristocrats of the mother country were typical English citizens.

The Democratic-Republican party also was led by the elite. Thomas Jefferson was a prominent Virginia planter, and he was one of the most brilliant Americans of the age. Even so, the party saw itself as the defender of the ordinary American, the small farmer, and the immigrant artisan.

There were many more immigrants and small farmers in the early United States than there were wealthy and educated men. As a result of this simple arithmetic, the Democratic-Republicans (by 1828, the Democrats) owned the presidency for the forty years following Jefferson's election in 1801. By the 1830s, the Democrats controlled both the Congress and the majority of other elected offices in the country.

The Federalist party quickly faded away, not even running a presidential candidate in the election of 1820. For a while, the Federalists stayed active on the state level in the Northeast, but by 1824 the party had all but disappeared even there.

The early Democrats succeeded for two main reasons: Most importantly, they appealed to a wide range of voters. They represented the interests of ordinary Americans from all over the country: small farmers of the South and the frontier, working men in the northern cities, and local merchants in every region. When it came to winning votes, this gave them a big advantage over the Federalists, who were seen mostly as the party of the northeastern elite.

The second reason for the Democratic party's success was its organization. Starting under Jefferson, it developed institutions to help Democratic candidates win elections, to use the power of the government once they were in office, and then to get themselves reelected. In short, the Democrats became a real political party, not just a collection of people who more or less agreed with each other.

A good example of these Democratic Party institutions was the party congressional caucus. (In those days, there were no Congresswomen. Women could not even vote.) Democratic Congressmen got together often to plan ways to benefit the party and themselves. For several years, they chose the party's candidate for President. Having the caucus make the choice guaranteed that the candidate would be someone who would appeal to voters across the country, someone the Democrats in Congress could work with once he was in office.

The early Democratic-Republican Presidents often joined with the caucus to choose their successors. In this way, Jefferson chose James Madison to follow him, and the caucus agreed with his choice. Madison, in turn, picked James Monroe, and the caucus agreed again. Monroe easily defeated the last Federalist candidate in 1816, and he was virtually unopposed for reelection in 1820.

▶ Splits in the Party

Without the Federalists to oppose them, the Democratic-Republicans began to produce opponents from inside their own party. When Monroe was ready to leave office in 1824, he chose his secretary of the Treasury, William H. Crawford, to succeed him. As usual, the caucus agreed with the President's choice. There were at least three other Democrats who wanted to be President, and each of them had his own supporting faction. These three men attacked the caucus system of nominating a candidate as too undemocratic. Congressmen should not be deciding who should run for President, they declared. Let the people choose.

Three powerful men decided to do battle with Monroe's choice. They were Senator Andrew Jackson, Democratic Speaker of the House of Representatives Henry Clay, and Monroe's own secretary of State, John Quincy Adams. The four-way election was extremely close.

In those days, people did not vote for President directly. Instead, they voted for people to participate in the electoral college, whose members would make the choice for them. Some members of the electoral college were chosen by the direct votes of citizens, some by state legislatures. Today we vote for the President directly. The electoral college still exists, but its members are always expected to vote the way the people in their state voted. In the 1820s, however, they were more or less free to pick whomever they wanted. Jackson won more votes in the electoral college than did any of the other candidates, but not enough to make him President.

According to the Constitution, it was now up to the House of Representatives to name a winner. The House picked John Quincy Adams, the maverick son of the last Federalist President, John Adams. John Quincy Adams was the head of a New England faction of the Democratic party known as the National Republicans, who favored a strong government role in developing the young country.

Jackson and his supporters were outraged; they felt that the presidency had been stolen from them.

Clay and Adams, they insisted, had made a "corrupt bargain" to steal the presidency.[1] Within a year, Jackson had left the Senate and had launched a new campaign for President. He won the office in 1828, soundly defeating Adams by more than two votes to one in the electoral college.

The election of 1840 marked the first major split in the Democratic party, but it would be far from the last. The Democratic party has been the most effective and long-lasting political organization in American history, but it has never been unified. There have always been factions among the Democrats, factions that are sometimes as hostile to each other as they are to rival parties.

▶ "The Party of the Common Man"

After Jefferson, the most famous Democratic President of the nineteenth century was Andrew Jackson, who took office in 1829. Nicknamed "Old Hickory," Jackson was a tremendously popular figure. He was a victorious general, a hero of the Indian Wars and the War of 1812. A self-declared champion of democracy, he appealed to the ordinary American, the hardworking farmer or frontiersman who owned little property and worked with his hands.

Jackson would have almost as much effect on the Democratic party as Thomas Jefferson, who founded the party and established it as a major force in American politics. "Old Hickory" transformed Jefferson's Democratic-Republicans into the Democrats, pure and simple—the party of the common man.

Andrew Jackson, known as "Old Hickory," transformed the Democratic party into "the party of the common man."

Just how common Jackson's backers were was demonstrated when he threw open the White House in 1829 for a celebration of his inauguration. Thousands of people showed up for the big party. They were very different from the respectable gentlemen and ladies who had attended previous inaugural balls. They were, in the words of one alarmed witness, "a rabble, a mob, of boys, negros, women, children, scrambling, fighting, romping . . . Ladies fainted, men were seen with bloody noses and such a scene of confusion took place as is impossible to describe."[2]

There were no bodyguards or police to keep order, and even the President himself was "nearly pressed to death & almost suffocated and torn to pieces by the people in their eagerness to shake hands." Jackson quickly escaped through an unmobbed exit, but others were less fortunate. Many of "those who got in could not get out by the door again, but had to scramble out of windows."[3]

The political descendants of the Federalists were appalled by news of the riotous doings in the White House. This was clearly a new kind of President, with a new kind of party behind him. Politics in America would never again be the gentleman's game it had been when Washington, Jefferson, and Adams had occupied the White House.

▶ "To the Victor Belong the Spoils"

Jackson did not want his government to be run by the highly educated, elite easterners who had filled most major government jobs in the past. Instead, he thought that the people's government should be run by common people, the kind who had supported and voted for him. To this end, he filled government positions with his supporters, that is, with Democrats. The Democrats had won the election, and Jackson believed that they deserved to reap the benefits.

In his inaugural address, Jackson announced that he would rotate federal jobs, removing officeholders appointed by earlier Presidents and putting his own people in their place.

Jackson did not invent the practice of awarding federal government posts to political friends. Virtually every President since Washington had done that. Jackson was the first to do it so openly and on such a grand scale, and he defended the practice as a way of making the federal government more democratic.

Conquering armies traditionally plunder the countries they invade, taking the defeated nation's food, gold, and other wealth at will. This booty is called the spoils of war. In politics, the conquering party finds itself in control of a variety of government jobs and government contracts. "To the victor," declared Senator William L. Marcy, "belong the spoils."[4] From then on, Jackson's policy was known as the spoils system.

Every victorious political party since Jackson has used the spoils system to one degree or another. Patronage—the awarding of government jobs to political supporters and friends—has been an important key to the control and influence of the party in power. By appointing party members to important offices, politicians in power ensure that the jobs are filled with people who are committed to the policies of the dominant party.

Patronage also is a way for the party in power to reward people who have helped to win the election. This not only assures that the people rewarded stay loyal to the party, it encourages others to support the party and to work for its victory in future elections.

By the end of the nineteenth century, the spoils system was widely attacked as corrupt. A law was passed to bring many federal jobs under the Civil Service Commission, an agency that is supposed to fill jobs by merit instead of by political loyalty. Nonetheless, many important jobs are still filled by political appointment, and Presidents and political parties still use these appointments to cement their power.

The Republicans

The Republicans call themselves the GOP. These initials stand for the Grand Old Party. Like a lot of other terms in politics, however, this nickname is misleading. The "grand old party" is, in fact, the younger of the two major parties. It was founded in 1854 by a mixture of northern Democrats, Whigs, and others opposed to the spread of slavery.

▶ The Whigs

The Whig party was united primarily by opposition to Andrew Jackson and the Democrats. They mocked Jackson as a would-be "King Andrew," and took the name Whig because that was the name of the British party that opposed the English monarchy. They supported the national bank, and were angered by what they saw as Jackson's high-handed attacks on it. They agreed about little else.

The Whigs did succeed in winning the White House from the Democrats in 1840, but only with a candidate who seemed almost more like a Democrat than the Democratic candidate did. Although William Henry Harrison had been born to a wealthy Virginia family, he was sold to the voters as a man of the frontier who had lived in a log cabin and had farmed his own land. In short, his public image was much like that of the hated Old Hickory himself.

Like Jackson, Harrison was a victorious military general who had won fame fighting in the War of 1812. He had fought the great Shawnee leader Tecumseh in the battle of Tippecanoe, and crushed a combined force of Native Americans and British in the Battle of the Thames. Harrison's running mate, John Tyler, was an ex-Democrat. Even the campaign slogan the Whigs shouted at their rallies— "Tippecanoe and Tyler too!"—had a Democratic, common-man ring to it.

Although the Democrats soon won back the White House, the Whigs continued to compete with them for the next two decades. They even elected another President, Zachary Taylor, in 1849.

Although the Whigs only won two presidential elections, there were four Whig Presidents. That was because Whig Presidents proved astonishingly unhealthy. Both Harrison and Taylor died soon after taking office, and they were succeeded by their Vice

For a time in the first half of the nineteenth century, the Whigs were a major party. This cartoon lampoons their practice of running military leaders for President. The skulls were prophetic. The only two Whigs to be elected — William Henry Harrison and Zachary Taylor — both died during their first years in office.

Presidents, John Tyler and Millard Fillmore. The party itself was also short lived, virtually disappearing from the political scene by 1854. The real long-term threat to the Democrats would come not from the Whigs but from the Republicans.

▶ Republicans and the Slavery Issue

Slavery was the greatest single political issue of the nineteenth century. It divided the country along economic, geographical, and moral lines, and it threatened to tear the country apart for decades. In order to keep the nation together, an uneasy balance had to be kept between the slave states and the free states, where slavery was outlawed. This assured that neither the proslavery nor antislavery forces could gain control of the Congress.

The shaky balance was upset by the Kansas-Nebraska Act of 1854, which established two vast new territories in the West. It allowed the settlers who flocked west to decide whether these territories would be slave or free. The result was bloody conflict in the new territories, and political upheaval throughout the nation.

The Democratic party had most of its strength in the South, so its members tended to support slavery. The Whigs, on the other hand were split over the issue of slavery and over the question of what should be done about the new territories. Although slavery was the big political issue of the day, neither major party stood squarely against its spread. This left a great political vacuum, which was quickly filled by a new party that called itself the Republican party.

The formal birth of the Republican party occurred at a meeting in the little town of Ripon, Wisconsin, on March 20, 1854. Although it had no support at all in the South, the Republican party swept across the North like a tidal wave, and it washed away the Whigs in the process.

The very year the party was founded, the Republicans won control of the House of Representatives. Two years later, they took eleven states in the presidential election of 1856, while the Whigs won only one state. The Republican candidate in that election was the dashing John Charles Frémont, who had led the rebellion against Spain that had made California a state a few years before. Four years later, the Republicans nominated their second presidential candidate, a tall homespun lawyer from Illinois named Abraham Lincoln.

Lincoln is now regarded by almost everyone as one of the greatest American Presidents, if not the greatest of them all. In his own time, however, he was at least as much despised as he was admired. He was hated in the South, and he was bitterly controversial even in the North. Democrats considered him a reckless warmonger, while many Republicans considered him weak and untrustworthy. His election led to the Civil War, and ultimately to the freeing of the slaves. Then, as the war was ending, Lincoln was assassinated. He was succeeded by his Vice President, Andrew Johnson, and then by a series of Republican Presidents.

Following a policy of Radical Reconstruction

A meeting held in this small house in Ripon, Wisconsin, on March 20, 1854, launched the Republican party.

after the war, the Republican administrations sent federal troops to the South to enforce the rights of the freed slaves. This made the party even more hated by southern whites than it had been before. For the next one hundred years, southern whites would regard the Republicans as the party of the hated North and would identify themselves more firmly than ever with the rival Democrats.

▶ Policies

Aside from the bitter hostilities inflamed by the war and by Reconstruction, nineteenth-century Republicans and Democrats favored many of the same policies. They shared a similar devotion to the principles laid out in the Declaration of Independence, a similar commitment to the United States Constitution, and a similar vision of individual liberty. Both parties favored encouraging businesspeople, farmers, and other settlers to move west, planting the American flag all the way to the Pacific Ocean.

The main differences between the parties had to do with money and business. The Republicans identified themselves with the big business interests that were strongest in the North. In control of Congress, they enacted high tariffs, taxes on foreign goods, to protect northern manufacturers. The Democrats, on the other hand, wanted low tariffs that would make foreign goods cheaper for Americans to buy and would encourage foreign countries not to put their own tariffs on the produce of American farmers.

The Republicans wanted the United States dollar

In 1856, the new Republican Party put forth its very first presidential candidate, the dashing young hero John C. Frémont.

tied firmly to gold. Paper money, they believed, should always be exchangeable for gold. No more money should be printed than there was gold to pay for it. This fought inflation, and it helped to preserve the value of the property owned by wealthy companies and individuals.

The Democrats, on the other hand, wanted as much money printed as possible. This reduced the value of each dollar, but the cheaper the money was, the easier it was to get it. Cheap money helped poor farmers and other ordinary Americans to borrow in order to keep their farms and businesses going in hard times.

Both parties wanted to promote business activity, but the Democrats of the late nineteenth century wanted some government regulation of business. This was the age of the so-called "robber barons," wealthy men who used cutthroat methods to build great fortunes in steel, oil, coal, and other industries. They used unscrupulous tactics to drive competing companies out of business. They paid poverty wages to workers, including children, who slaved away for twelve and more hours each day in unsafe conditions. When the workers protested, goons were hired to attack them.

The Democrats, who were getting more and more of their members from the immigrants who were flooding into the country to work in American factories, wanted to put some limits on these practices. The Republicans, on the other hand, turned a blind eye to all this. They ignored the plight

Abraham Lincoln first gained fame debating the Democrat Stephen A. Douglas (seated to Lincoln's left) as a candidate for the Senate from Illinois in 1858. If he had won, he might never have become the first—and perhaps the greatest—Republican President two years later.

of the workers, and they favored policies that turned over large quantities of formerly public land to private businesses.

The biggest business of all in nineteenth-century America was the railroad industry, which got the biggest benefits from Republican policies. The Republican Congress granted the railroads not only free right-of-way across the continent, but twenty square miles of land for every mile of track they laid.

Although slavery was no longer an issue after the Civil War, the Republican party remained a powerful force in American politics. For a long time after the Civil War, in fact, it would be the more powerful of the two parties, electing five of the next six Presidents.

The Golden Age
of Party Power

By the end of the Civil War, it was clear that there were only two major political parties in the United States. The Whigs had died out, and no other party was strong enough to threaten Republican and Democratic control of Congress and the presidency. If there had been any doubt about the power of the two parties, it was removed in 1877, when the two major parties bypassed the voters and decided for themselves who should be President.

The election of 1876 was the closest and the most violent that the young country had ever seen. For the first time in sixteen years, the Republicans were in serious danger of losing the presidency. Their war hero, President Ulysses S. Grant, was stepping down without running for reelection after two scandal-ridden terms in office. Several members of his administration had been caught making corrupt deals, taking bribes, or stealing from the federal government. On the other hand, the Democrats were fired up by the prospect of regaining the presidency and repairing the damage the Civil War had done to their status as a national party.

Both candidates in the election—the Republican, Rutherford B. Hayes, and the Democrat, James Tilden—claimed to be political reformers. Their supporters, though, ran the dirtiest and most bloody campaign in United States history. Controlling the Army, the Republicans used federal troops to frighten Democratic voters in the South. Meanwhile, the Ku Klux Klan and other white supremacist organizations launched a wave of lynchings and beatings to keep black voters away from the polls.

For the first time since before the Civil War, it looked as though the Democrats might have a chance to win the presidency, and that is exactly what happened. Tilden got 4,300,590 votes, while Hayes got only 4,036,298, but each party submitted different totals for three southern states, and one electoral vote in Oregon was in dispute as well.

According to the Constitution, it was up to the House of Representatives to decide who had won. In reality, it was up to the politicians—the leadership of the two major parties—to make a deal.

Although their candidate actually had won the election, the Democrats agreed to let the Republican, Hayes, take the presidency by giving him all the

A campaign song for Rutherford B. Hayes (left), the reformer who became President in the bloodiest campaign in United States history.

disputed votes. In return, the Republicans gave the Democrats almost everything else they wanted. Among other things, they let the Democrats hand out the federal patronage jobs in Democratic parts of the country, and they removed the federal troops from the South.

Radical Reconstruction was over, and before long African Americans in the South would lose the rights that federal troops had protected, including the right to vote. The Republicans had traded these civil rights away in return for the presidency. It was a shameful deal, but it demonstrated more clearly than ever before that the two main parties were in control of political life in the United States. For nearly a century, these parties would keep that control firmly in their hands.

▶ The Machines

The late nineteenth century and the first half of the twentieth saw a golden age of party power. During this time, each of the two parties built up its own city, county, and state organizations, known as political machines. The most effective of these machines showed the parties at their best and their worst, and showed their power at its strongest and crudest.

A party machine that was strong enough to elect its own candidates to local government at will became a kind of government itself. Because the machine controlled the people it put into office, the power of the government became the power of the machine.

Each machine was run by a boss; he (it was always a man) was the real political power in the community. Some, like Mayor Richard J. Daley, for years the Democratic boss of Chicago, were high elected officials. Other bosses held only minor positions, or no public office at all, working entirely in the background. The bosses acted through armies of lieutenants who did the machines' work in the neighborhoods, or wards, as they were called in Chicago.

The machines could control local governments because they controlled local elections. The bosses handpicked candidates who would cooperate with them, and party workers assured the candidates' election. The machines were highly organized and extremely effective political operations that were very good at persuading voters to elect machine candidates. They had ward healers, or precinct captains, in every neighborhood and in virtually every block in the city to get out the vote.

The bosses did not always rely on legitimate voters alone. When elections looked dangerously close, some bosses were not above sending out goons to intimidate opposition voters or to stuff ballot boxes to make sure that their candidates won. In some big cities, it was common for the names of dead people to remain on the lists of registered voters, and for repeat voters to cast ballots using the names of the dead people, years after they had been buried.

With its own people in office, the machine used

the government's power and the money collected in taxes to shore up machine power. The machines were built on a local version of the spoils system Andrew Jackson had perfected at the national level. They handed out patronage jobs to loyal party workers, and they awarded valuable contracts for city projects to businesses that contributed to the party.

At one time or another, every United States city of any size had its own political machine. The machine was either Republican or Democratic, depending on which party was strongest in that particular community.

Some cities had two machines, one for each party. At times, these machines would struggle for control of a city. The battles between them could be fierce, and sometimes bloody. In 1894, for example, a gun battle broke out in Troy, New York, between repeat voters working for the Democratic machine and local police who supported the Republican-controlled city government. Three people were killed in the fighting, but no one was arrested.

In other cases, the machines would make a kind of peace with each other. Instead of fighting over the spoils, they would share them. The Republicans might take over a city government, for instance, while the Democrats were free to run the county. In one rural Kentucky county, the two parties traded control of government institutions every few years. This way, both sides were satisfied, and no one got hurt.

The machines were like local branches of the

national party, but they were also independent organizations, doing pretty much what the local bosses wanted them to do. Because they controlled the votes in their own localities, the national party depended on them more than they depended on it. National political leaders would court the local bosses, hoping for their backing in the next election.

▶ Boss Rule in the Big Cities

Machines existed all over the country. They ran rural counties in states like Texas and Kentucky, as well as city governments in virtually every state. Although machines existed almost everywhere, they are most often identified with the big cities. That is because the biggest and most powerful machines were based there, and for a good reason. The most people, the most votes, and the most patronage jobs were in the big cities.

The early machines were particularly strong in East Coast cities where the great waves of immigrants came into the country in the late nineteenth and early twentieth centuries. These immigrants were the foundation on which many of the machines were built.

Workers for the machines haunted the docks where the immigrants arrived. They welcomed the newcomers to America and won their loyalty by offering them help and jobs. In return, the immigrants voted the way the machines wanted them to. Building on this base, the machines usually had enough votes to win any election.

The first, most powerful, and most long-lived of

As this political cartoon suggests, major party machines were "Siamese twins" of corruption in many big cities.

all the machines was the Democratic machine in New York City. It was originally founded in the 1780s as the local branch of a national patriotic organization, the Tammany societies, and it became known simply as Tammany, or Tammany Hall. Most of the other Tammany groups soon died out, but the New York chapter grew steadily bigger and stronger. By the 1820s, it was firmly identified with the Democratic party, and with the cause of the Irish and the other poor immigrants who were then flooding into the city.

Tammany backed Andrew Jackson in the presidential election of 1824, and shared lavishly in the spoils when he won. From that time on, it played an important part in national, local, and state politics.

Tammany's fortunes and its reputation shifted many times over the years. As the country's biggest and most influential machine, it was a frequent target of political reformers. Under one infamous boss, William Marcy Tweed, it became a national symbol for fraud and corruption in the 1860s. On the other hand, under the likes of Charles Murphy, the boss who took over in 1902, it was sometimes regarded as one of the most effective machines in the country.

▶ The Machines and the Presidency

The machines were local and state institutions, but they were important in national politics as well. They controlled millions of votes in the big cities. This made the bosses major powers within the national political parties. When they spoke, other party leaders and the party's candidates listened.

Many national political leaders from both parties—including representatives, senators, and even Presidents—began their careers under the wing of a local boss. President Harry Truman, for example, was a protégé of Tom Pendergast, the Democratic boss of Kansas City, Missouri.

The machines did more than groom national leaders; they helped to elect them, too. In 1896, Matthew Quay, the Republican boss of Pennsylvania, scoffed when President Benjamin Harrison thanked God for his election. It was not God who had won the presidency for Harrison, insisted Quay; it was he and his fellow Republican bosses. What's more, they had "approached the gates of the penitentiary to do it."[1]

John F. Kennedy might never have been President if it were not for the power of two Democratic machines. Kennedy's 1960 election was decided by extremely close votes in Illinois and Texas. Illinois was won by a heavy turnout of Democratic voters in Chicago. Texas was won by a narrow margin of votes in a rural Texas county where the machine was fiercely loyal to Kennedy's vice presidential running mate, Lyndon Johnson.

▶ Corruption

The political machines did a lot of good. Without them, generations of immigrants would have had a much harder time adjusting to life in America. They provided jobs for many people who would have lived in poverty, or turned to crime, if these jobs had not existed.

The machines often were good at the day-to-day business of government; they got things done. Under Daley's Democratic machine, for example, Chicago won a reputation for being "the city that works." The buses and subways ran on time, the potholes in the streets were repaired quickly, and the garbage was always picked up.

The country paid a heavy price for the good that the machines did; that price was corruption. The machines won and kept their power by unethical, and often illegal, means. They kept a stranglehold on the political nominating process. This kept many potentially excellent public servants from running for office, and it reduced the choices available to voters. In addition, they handed out government jobs to their political cronies, frequently ignoring others who deserved the jobs more.

Many machine politicians filled their own pockets with taxpayers' money. "I work for my pocket all the time," one Tammany Hall operator declared.[2] The bosses and their henchmen got rich by taking kickbacks, illegal payments given to officeholders as rewards for getting a share of the business done with the government. The machine would see to it that a local contractor got the job of paving the city streets. In return, the contractor would secretly give back a healthy chunk of the money he received to the machine workers who arranged the deal.

Worst of all, some machines were connected with organized crime. During Prohibition (1919–1933), when alcohol was outlawed, many of the machines were allied with the bootleggers. Later on, they cooperated with the Mafia and other large criminal organizations. In return for money and other favors, some machine-run city governments ignored the bootlegging, extortion, drug dealing, prostitution, and other large-scale criminal operations of the mobs.

▶ Reform

Reformers attacked the machines for their corruption. They launched campaigns in favor of honest elections and clean government. They fielded candidates to run against the stooges picked by the bosses, and those reform candidates frequently won. The machines did not give up power easily, however. Many of the victorious reformers were no better than the machines at running the government, and sometimes they were worse. As often as not, the machines swept back into power in the next election.

In the end, the reformers won. More and more voters got fed up with the almost open corruption of the party machines. The immigrant waves that had been the base of the machine's power began drying up. The grandchildren and great-grandchildren of immigrants did not need to rely on the machines to find them jobs, or to tell them whom to vote for. They decided for themselves.

The reformers were helped by laws in many states that required parties to choose candidates by primary elections. This took the power to handpick candidates away from the bosses. Other laws took the power to hand out government jobs away from the machine as well. They required that jobs be awarded on the basis of tests, not political favoritism.

Still other reform laws changed the way money was raised for political campaigns. They required parties and candidates to open up their books and to reveal where their money came from. This made it harder for machines to control the political purse strings, and to hide bribes, kickbacks, and other under-the-table payoffs.

The development of television also had a role in deflating the influence of the machines. Candidates who use television in their campaigns do not have to rely on political machines to reach voters. They can appeal to them directly, in the voters' own living rooms.

▶ What's Left of the Machines

Political machines still exist. In a sense, every local, county, and state party organization is a kind of machine. Some of these machines still have a lot of power. In places where the vast majority of voters are either Democratic or Republican, the party organizations still can determine who will run for office and who will get elected. Today's machines are not nearly as powerful as those of yesterday.

What is true of the machines is true of the political parties behind the machines. The same reforms that sapped the power of the machines deflated the power of the national political parties as well.

Even presidential candidates no longer need the parties as much as before. They do not have to rely on party bosses—or even the national Democratic or Republican party organization—to support them for nomination. They can run in direct primaries in many states, appealing to the voters directly on television. If they arrive at the national convention with enough delegates won in the primaries, the national party organization has to nominate them whether it wants to or not.

Most people think that the decline of party power is a good thing. The people have gained the power that the parties lost. Politics is much more democratic—and more honest—than it used to be.

Others are not sure that the decline in the power of political party organizations is entirely good. They point out that the bosses and other party professionals often made good choices of national candidates. Theodore and Franklin Roosevelt, Harry Truman, Dwight Eisenhower, and John Kennedy were all chosen with the backing of powerful political machines.

No matter.

Whether for good or bad, the golden age of the political machine—and of the political party—is long past. This does not mean that the parties are no longer important, although they are not as powerful as they used to be. Their organizations no longer control the votes of whole cities or states, but the Democratic and Republican parties still dominate American political life.

Changing Times, Changing Positions

One of the most important purposes of a political party is to stand for something. A party represents an ideology, a combination of ideas and values that define what the party believes in, and what it wants for the country.

Party ideology is not constant, however. Over the years, the Republicans and Democrats have stood for different things. Changing times and new perspectives cause the parties to change their opinions, and to look for new solutions.

Sometimes the parties even switch positions, with each one taking up a position the other supported in the past. In many ways, a time-traveling Democrat from the days of Andrew Jackson would be more comfortable in the Republican party today.

A Republican from early in the twentieth century might be happier as a modern Democrat.

▶ Economic Policy

In the 1830s and 1840s, it was Andrew Jackson and the Democrats who argued for "laissez-faire." That is, they wanted the government to stay out of business affairs. The Whigs, on the other hand, wanted government to play a major role in economic affairs and to stimulate business activity. They believed that the government should take steps to keep the economy healthy and to make sure that there would be enough goods and money to go around.

Before very long, however, the Democrats and the Whigs were arguing over how much the government should do to help private businesses. The issue between them was not whether the government should get involved in business affairs, but how it should get involved.

When the Republicans appeared on the scene, the new party allied itself with the interests of big business. Like the old-time Democrats, they claimed to support the laissez-faire policy. At the same time, they promoted policies that helped the big railroads and the other giant industries that were springing up like mushrooms in the nineteenth century. The Democrats, meanwhile, championed the interests of the small businesses that were often at odds with the giant companies.

Despite the Republicans' support of big business, it was a Republican President who first took up the challenge of bringing big business under government regulation. In his inaugural address, Theodore Roosevelt declared that the growing size and power of the big corporations should be "supervised and within reasonable limits controlled" by the government.[1] Roosevelt became famous as a trust-buster. He was the first President to bring the huge corporations under the regulation of the federal government in peacetime.

Within a few decades, however, the Republicans were leading the opposition to government regulation of business. In the 1930s, they fought tooth and nail against the efforts of a Democratic President, Franklin D. Roosevelt, to regulate and control business activity. In the century between Jackson and the second Roosevelt, then, the Democrats had completely abandoned laissez-faire, and the Republicans had taken it as their own.

▶ Deficit Spending

Over the next fifty years, the parties did a similar flip-flop over the issue of the national debt. A Democrat, Franklin Roosevelt, won the presidency during the Great Depression, when the country was in economic trouble. He quickly launched the New Deal—a multitude of ambitious and expensive government programs to combat the Depression.

Because most Americans had little money to pay the taxes that would pay for these programs, the government was forced into deficit spending: It had to borrow money and go into debt. Deficit spending used to finance the New Deal lifted the national debt from about $16 billion in 1930 to over $40 billion by 1940.

The Republicans complained bitterly that this spending was irresponsible. The Democrats, they complained, were smothering the economy and saddling future generations with debt. Their complaints were silenced, however, by the exploding bombs of World War II. The borrowing needed to pay for that vast military effort made the debt caused by the New Deal look small. During the war, the national debt skyrocketed to nearly $260 billion.

This war spending was supported by both parties. After the war both parties hoped to get the country out of debt, but this proved hard to do. The debt continued to rise slowly under both Republican and Democratic administrations in the 1950s and 1960s. It had climbed to $370 billion by 1970, when it took off again, soaring to over $900 billion by 1980.

The Republicans insisted that this enormous debt was the Democrats' fault, and that something must be done. The debt must be paid off, and the first step was for the government to balance the budget, to spend no more each year than it collected in taxes.

There had not been a balanced budget since the late 1960s, under President Lyndon Johnson, a Democrat. Even so, the Republicans blamed the Democrats for the deficit, because the Democrats had controlled both the White House and the Congress for most of the 1960s and some of the 1970s as well.

The Republicans bitterly attacked the Democrats as the party of "tax and spend." The country was drowning in debt, they said. If something were not done to end the deficit spending, the economy surely would collapse. The Democrats argued that the spending had been necessary to fight the war in Vietnam and to fight poverty at home. Besides, the debt was not all that great, compared to the size of the national economy.

In 1980, a Republican, Ronald Reagan, was swept into the presidency promising to balance the budget within a few years, and to pay off the national debt. He failed. Despite his promise to eliminate the debt, he called for spending larger and larger amounts of money on the military, and he called for lowering tax rates at the same time. The Congress followed much of his advice, adding some increased social spending of its own, and the debt soared.

Despite his promise to balance the budget, President Reagan never presented a balanced budget to Congress. He was followed in office by another Republican, George Bush, who never presented a balanced budget either. In each of the twelve years of these Republican presidencies, from 1980 to 1992, the Democratic Congress actually reduced the deficit in each Republican budget, although not by much. It seems clear that both parties played major roles in unbalancing the budget even further in the 1980s.

By the campaign of 1992, the Democrats were demanding an end to the deficits and a paydown of

In the 1980s, President Ronald Reagan helped the Republican party break up the Democratic coalition formed by FDR, capturing many traditionally Democratic working-class and southern voters.

the debt. The Republicans had to admit that under their policies the debt had soared to more than $4 trillion—more than four times what it had been under the last Democratic President. It had climbed faster and higher under Republican leadership than it ever had under Democratic rule.

Now it was the Republicans who insisted that the debt was not as important as the Democrats claimed it was. The huge military spending was needed to discourage the Soviet Union, and ultimately to cause its collapse, they said. Now, given a healthy economy, many Republicans insisted, the country would soon grow its way out of debt.

The flip-flop was complete.

▶ Vietnam

Sometimes the differences between the two parties seem to be greater than they are. This was true when it came to the war in Vietnam. The war was extremely controversial. American involvement there took place under both Republican and Democratic administrations, and it lasted for nearly a quarter of a century.

It began under President Eisenhower, a Republican, and was extended under his successor, John Kennedy, a Democrat. In the election of 1964, the Republican candidate, Barry Goldwater, was a hawk. He demanded that the United States escalate the war. The Democratic President, Lyndon Johnson, on the other hand, campaigned almost as a peace candidate. Although he did not call for immediate United States withdrawal from Vietnam, he seemed to promise an early end to the fighting. He assured the voters that "We still seek no wider war."[2] As a result, most of those Americans who opposed the war, along with many who supported it, voted for him. Johnson won in a landslide.

Despite his peaceful campaign talk, Johnson quickly escalated the war once the election was over. He doubled the number of American troops stationed in Vietnam within a year, and doubled them again the year after that. By the time he left office, he had expanded United States involvement from seventy-five thousand troops to over four hundred and sixty thousand.[3]

The campaign of 1968 was almost a reversal of the 1964 campaign. This time it was the Republican candidate, Richard Nixon, who seemed to offer the best promise of peace. The Democratic candidate, Hubert Humphrey, had been Johnson's Vice President, and supported his policy of escalation. Nixon, on the other hand, claimed to have a plan to end American involvement in Vietnam, although he could not say what it was without tipping off the enemy North Vietnamese.

Nixon won, but, like the Democrat before him, he proceeded to escalate the war, even extending it into Vietnam's neighbor, Cambodia. It would be nearly five years before America's involvement in the war was finally ended.

Vietnam was not a typical case of the parties' flip-flopping positions. In reality, the leaders of both parties seemed to favor escalation of the war, but they did not make their positions clear. Instead, the party out of power tried to make it seem that it differed more with the party in power than it really did.

▶ Changing Constituencies

In changing their positions on issues, the parties change their constituencies—the people they represent—as well. A party that favors policies promoting big business will be supported by big business. A party that favors the interests of factory workers will be supported by those workers.

Which comes first? Do the parties change their positions because their ideas change, or because they want to appeal to new constituents? Or both?

The most massive shifts of constituents have occurred in the South. For almost the entire century after the Civil War, the Democrats held a virtual lock on the votes of most white southerners. Their hold was so strong that the states of the old confederacy were referred to as the "solid South." They were so solidly Democratic that the Republicans hardly bothered to campaign there.

The Republicans, meanwhile, had a similar lock on the votes of African Americans all across the country. The Republican party, after all, had been founded to limit the spread of slavery, and a Republican President had presided over the war that freed the slaves. African Americans saw the Republicans—the party of Lincoln—as the party that represented their rights and interests, so Republican political candidates got most of their votes.

That situation began to change dramatically after

a Democrat, Franklin Roosevelt, won the presidency in 1932, in the midst of the Great Depression. Under Roosevelt, the Democrats passed measures designed to help the poor survive the hard economic times. The Republicans opposed many of these measures. Most African Americans of the time were poor, and many appreciated the Democrats' efforts on their behalf.

Constituents have many different interests. African Americans had certain concerns because of their color, but they had other concerns because they were poor. Their history drew them toward the Republicans, but their economic needs drew them to the Democrats. More and more, their different interests began to merge, as the Democratic party adopted new policies that brought African Americans closer to the mainstream of American society.

It was a Democratic President, Harry Truman, who ordered that black soldiers in the United States Army should serve side by side with whites. This was something no Republican President had done. It was two other Democratic Presidents, John Kennedy and Lyndon Johnson, who presided over the end to legal racial segregation. It was a Democratic Congress that passed the 1964 Civil Rights Act, the bill that finally guaranteed African Americans the citizens' rights they had been promised after the Civil War.

Why did the Democratic party do these things? It did them partly because Democratic leaders believed they were the right things to do. Harry Truman knew that African-American troops had

Franklin Delano Roosevelt was the Democrat who would be elected President four times. Uniting minorities, big city dwellers, and rural southerners under one banner, he forged a solid Democratic majority that lasted for over half a century.

fought and died as bravely as any white troops in World War II. He honestly believed that it was wrong to ask them to do these things in segregated units.

The Democrats did not help African Americans just because they believed it was right. They saw a political advantage in what they were doing. The Democrats wanted the African Americans' vote, and, for a time, they won the allegiance of the majority of both white and black voters in the South.

Eventually, however, the Republicans saw a chance to grab the votes of white southerners. Many whites were upset by the gains that blacks were making in the South, and they were unhappy with the Democrats for helping them. They had always supported the Democrats, and they felt betrayed. Nonetheless, they had been Democrats for generations, and were reluctant to change.

The Republicans' chance to win the white South came when the Vietnam War heated up in the late 1960s. The war was dividing public opinion across the country, but most white southerners were inclined to support it. Although the Democratic party officially supported the war, most of the political opposition to the war came from liberal Democrats. Many white southerners began to see the Democratic party as weak when it came to supporting the war.

Under the leadership of President Richard Nixon, the Republicans seized their opportunity. Nixon launched what he called his "Southern strategy." He appealed both to the traditional patriotism of southern voters and to the resentment that many white southerners felt toward the Democrats for their support of the rights of blacks. In the process, he destroyed whatever was left of the loyalty those African Americans had felt toward the Republican party since the Civil War.

As a result, the two parties exchanged millions of their constituents. The once "solid South" now tends to vote for Republican candidates in presidential elections, and the great majority of African Americans vote for Democrats.

Where the Parties Stand Today

The Democratic and Republican parties set the terms of political debate in the United States. Their positions on major issues define the range of mainstream opinion in American politics.

In general, the Republicans are on the right wing of the political mainstream, and the Democrats are on the left. This means that the Republicans are more conservative on economic and social issues, while the Democrats are more liberal. What this means in terms of actual positions will become clear later in this chapter.

▶ Party Platforms

Each party proclaims the positions it takes on important issues in its platform, which is a document that the party writes every fourth year at its national convention. Each position in the platform is called a plank. The planks are written by a committee of delegates to the convention. The members often argue bitterly over party positions. Most often, they work out a compromise. In the end, the platform is voted on by the entire convention.

The document is called a platform because the party's candidates are expected to "stand on" it in the upcoming election. That is, they are supposed to campaign on the issues it raises, and adopt the positions it takes as their own. Not all candidates stand on every plank of their party's platform, however. Even so, the final platform becomes the official statement of what the party stands for as an institution, no matter what individual members, or factions, of the party may believe.

Because they are writing campaign documents, the authors of platforms try to do two things: First, they try to appeal to voters, and second, they try to set the party apart from its opponents. The platforms are designed to give voters reasons to support the party, and to reject other parties.

Instead of spelling out detailed proposals, platforms tend to make general declarations of belief and principle. Because of this, some people dismiss the importance of party platforms because, they say, platforms are too vague and unspecific. Platforms are important, though, because they reveal a lot about how the parties see themselves, and what they want to represent.

▶ The Purpose of Government

"We believe our laws should reflect what makes our Nation prosperous and wholesome," Republicans declared in their 1992 platform. And what was that? "Faith in God, hard work, service to others, and limited government."[1]

That same year, the Democrats' platform proclaimed their belief in an "activist government," and in "the promise of opportunity, the strength of community, the dignity of work, and a decent life for senior citizens."[2]

These two declarations are revealing. In theory, at least, the Democratic party emphasizes the common interests of all American citizens, and looks to the government to promote those interests. The Republican party, on the other hand, emphasizes the efforts of individual citizens, and calls on the government to get out of their way.

In general, the Democratic party sees the federal government as a more important part of people's lives than does the Republican party. Democrats think of it as an agent for getting things done. They look for ways that government can help to make things better for people. Therefore, they tend to favor increased government action to protect the rights of the people, and new federal programs to ensure their well-being.

The Republicans, on the other hand, tend to distrust the federal government and to oppose most extensions of federal authority. They like to quote the first Republican President, Abraham Lincoln, who said:

> The legitimate object of Government is to do for a community of people what they need to have done, but cannot do, or cannot so well do, for themselves in their separate and individual capacities. But in all that people can do as well for themselves, Government ought not to interfere.

These differences are only relative, however. The Republicans do not oppose every proposed government program, and the Democrats do not support every one, either. On some issues, in fact, the Republicans actually support more federal power than do the Democrats. When it comes to expanding the federal government's police powers, for example, Republicans tend to favor even stronger measures to enforce law and order than the Democrats favor. This includes granting greater authority to federal agencies like the Drug Enforcement Administration, even though that means expanding the federal government's power.

▶ Party Positions on Some Key Issues

The positions described in this section are generalizations. They are not meant to represent the views of all Republicans or all Democrats. Instead, they give an idea of what most Republicans and most Democrats tend to believe. They are based on positions taken by prominent politicians from each party, and on the positions in the parties' recent platforms.

Family Values. Ever since the nomination of

Ronald Reagan in 1980, the Republicans have defined themselves as the party of what they call "family values." Although not all Republicans are Christians, many connect their devotion to "family values" with their belief in Christianity.

While the Republicans "support the courageous efforts of single-parent families to have a stable home," they insist that the "two-parent family still provides the best environment of stability, discipline, responsibility, and character."

They object to laws that, they claim, interfere with the rights of parents and families. These include welfare laws that provide more support to single parents than to married parents, and tax policies that make married couples living together pay more in taxes than the two of them would pay if each were single.

Democrats object when Republicans try to wrap themselves in the mantle of family values. They insist that the Democratic party supports family values, too, but that it does so in different ways. It promotes welfare and other programs that help poor and struggling families to support themselves and to stay together.

The Republicans, they charge, really only care about one kind of family—mother, father, and children, living together. The Democrats favor policies that help other kinds of families as well, including single parents and nonmarried couples, particularly those with children.

Some Democrats argue that gay and lesbian couples ought to be legally recognized as families. Most

Republicans, however, object to treating homosexual and other bonds as equal to the bond of what they consider to be the traditional family—one with two parents of opposite sexes. They believe that this undermines the stability and moral values that the society needs in order to prosper.

Education. The Republicans' emphasis on the authority of parents carries over into their education policies. "Schools," they say, "should teach [people to tell] right from wrong. They should reinforce parental authority, not replace it."

The Republicans want parents to have more opportunities to choose their children's schools than traditional public school systems allow. The more choice parents have, they say, the harder all schools will work to get more students. This, they say, will raise the quality of education in all the schools. Therefore, Republicans tend to support programs that allow parents to choose which public schools their children attend. Some support government help for parents who want to pay for private schools, including religious schools. "America needs public, private, and parochial schools," the Republican 1992 platform declared.

The Republicans are suspicious of several recent trends in public education. They consider most educational programs sponsored by the National Education Association and other teachers' organizations to be too liberal. They particularly object to sex education in the schools, and they oppose giving students information about birth control.

If anything, the Democrats put an even higher value on education than do the Republicans. "Education," proclaimed the Democratic platform in 1992, is "the core of our economy, democracy, and society." In general, the Democrats are more committed to the public education system than are the Republicans, and they are less in favor of supporting private schools.

The Democrats tend to support sex education and to encourage greater diversity within the schools. Where the Republicans emphasize the value of competition in raising the level of education, the Democrats emphasize the need to provide an education of equally high quality to all young people.

In general, the Democrats are suspicious of vouchers and other programs that give parents a choice of schools. They fear that a voucher system will inevitably take money away from the public schools that have the job of educating most children. Choice, they say, would create a two-level school system. Vouchers would be too small to pay for expensive schools. Well-to-do parents would send their children to good schools in pleasant surroundings, while the children of the poor would be left to struggle in "educational ghettoes" in their own impoverished neighborhoods.

Welfare. The Democratic party emphasizes the Constitution's call to "provide for the general welfare." Historically, Democrats have supported programs to help the unfortunate, and to raise the standard of living of the poor. Social Security, food stamps, AFDC (Aid to Families with Dependent Children), and Medicare were all Democratic measures.

The Republicans, on the other hand, are hostile to government programs they consider to be hand-outs. These are programs that take tax money from prosperous people to provide goods and services to others. They are particularly wary of welfare pro-grams designed to help the poor, the elderly, and the disabled. They complain that these programs are often misguided and wasteful.

Republicans do not automatically oppose all government aid to individuals, however. They do believe that society should provide what Ronald Reagan called a "safety net" to protect those who really cannot survive without government help, but they argue that the current social programs are too generous. They say that too many people find it easier to be on welfare than to get a job.

The Democrats believe that the Republicans overstate this problem of "welfare dependence." They insist that most people who receive welfare do need it. Nonetheless, in their 1992 platform, the Democrats moved closer toward the traditional Re-publican position, declaring that "no one who is able to work can stay on welfare forever," but still insist-ing that "no one who works should live in poverty."

Both parties favor reforming the current welfare system. They differ, however, in how they would reform it. The Democrats are more concerned with making sure that people who need help receive it.

The Republicans are more concerned with making sure that tax money is not spent on people who actually could help themselves.

Spending. The Republicans accuse the Democrats of being the party of "tax and spend." The Democrats, they claim, favor too much government spending, and raising taxes too high to pay for it. The Democrats respond that they actually favor less spending than do the Republicans. They point out that spending rose much faster under recent Republican Presidents than it did under Democrats.

In reality, the parties each tend to favor higher spending for different purposes. The enormous increase in spending under Ronald Reagan went primarily for advanced weapons and other military goods. The Democrats, on the other hand, tend to favor more spending on government social programs designed to help poor and middle-class people.

Taxation. The parties argue about how much money the government should spend, and what to spend it on, but both recognize that the government must spend a great deal of money, and that the money has to come from some kind of taxes. They differ, however, on how the money should be raised, and who should be taxed.

The Democrats believe that the tax system should be progressive. It should "[force] the rich to pay their fair share." The Democrats argue that the better off people are, the more they have benefited from American society, and the more they should contribute to it in return. Therefore, Democrats tend to support taxes that hit the rich more heavily, such as taxes on luxury goods like second homes and expensive automobiles, and a steeply progressive income tax.

Although some Republicans believe that taxes should be raised to pay off the national debt, most argue that tax rates should be kept as low as possible for everyone. Many also believe that taxes should be no higher on the rich than on anyone else. The more money wealthy people can keep for themselves, they argue, the more they will save and invest. These things help the United States economy and result in more jobs for more Americans.

Under Ronald Reagan, the Republicans flattened the income tax rates, lowering the percentage the rich have to pay to the same level as the upper middle class have to pay. Policies like these lead the Democrats to accuse the Republicans of being the "party of the rich."

The Democrats accuse the Republicans of trying to protect their wealthy contributors. They insist that progressive taxes hurt neither jobs nor the economy. The income tax was much more progressive in the 1950s and 1960s, they point out, when unemployment was lower and the economy more prosperous than it is today.

What They Have in Common. The two parties like to emphasize their differences, in order to persuade people to vote for them and against the other party. As we have seen in regard to Vietnam, however, the distinctions between Republicans and Democrats are not always as clear as they seem. Some Republicans tend to be more liberal on particular social issues than some Democrats tend to be. Some Democrats are more conservative on certain economic issues than are some Republicans.

Senator Mark Hatfield of Oregon got in trouble with many of his fellow Republicans when he provided the key vote that defeated the Balanced Budget Amendment to the Constitution in early 1995. All the other Republican senators supported the amendment, but Hatfield felt that it would be bad for the country. Although he was a part of the Democratic leadership in the House, David Bonior of Michigan has always opposed abortion, even though his party generally champions abortion rights.

Despite all the differences, both between the parties and within them, the two parties actually agree on many issues. Even their disagreements are often about the details of policies and programs, not about the policies themselves.

During the so-called Cold War (1954–1989), the Republicans charged that the Democrats were "soft" on Communism and weak on defense. The Republicans did sometimes call for larger defense budgets, and a greater variety of weapons systems, than did the Democrats. On the other hand, the Cold War was launched by a Democratic President, Harry Truman, and Democrats like John F. Kennedy were always among the most prominent Cold Warriors. Massive United States military buildups occurred under Presidents of both parties, including a Democrat, Lyndon Johnson, and a Republican, Ronald Reagan.

Since the end of the Cold War, the parties have struggled to find a new military policy. Both still support heavy spending on the military, and insist that the United States remain the strongest military power in the world. At the same time, both call for a reduction in the size of the United States armed forces following the end of the threat from the Soviet Union after its collapse in the early 1990s. They differ only on the size and speed of the reduction.

The Republicans typically call for a smaller reduction than do the Democrats. "Republicans call for a controlled defense drawdown, not a freefall," declared the 1992 Republican platform. Despite its desire to go slowly, the party boasted that the Republican President, George Bush, already had cut out a hundred weapons systems, and planned to eliminate one out of every four jobs in the armed forces.

The parties actually agree with each other on many—if not most—of the truly fundamental issues in American politics:

Both parties generally support the United States Constitution and the system of government it prescribes.

Both parties are willing to reduce America's massive arsenal of nuclear weapons, but both want the United States to stay the world's strongest nuclear power.

Both parties continue to complain about the

huge national debt, but neither has a plan for getting rid of it.

Both parties support welfare reform while calling for individuals to take more responsibility for their own well-being.

Both parties oppose the legalization of drugs.

Although the Republicans generally favor lower and flatter income taxes than do the Democrats, neither party wants to eliminate the income tax altogether.

The differences between the parties are often differences of degree. The specific positions they take on many issues depend more on which party is in power than on ideology. The party on the outside tends to attack the policies of the party in power, wherever they seem most vulnerable.

In the presidential election of 1992, for example, the Democratic challenger, Bill Clinton, attacked the Republican President, George Bush, on some key foreign policy issues involving human rights. He denounced Bush's granting of "most favored nation" status to China, in spite of the fact that China was committing massive human rights abuses. He also protested Bush's policy of returning refugees from the brutal military regime in Haiti to their own country. Yet when Clinton became President, he ordered that the Haitian refugees be returned, just as Bush had done. In addition, instead of taking away China's "most favored nation" status, he renewed it.

Who's Who

In political discussions, people often say, "I'm a Democrat," or "I'm a Republican." What does this really mean?

One thing it usually does not mean is that the person actually belongs to that political organization. In fact, it often means nothing more or less than that they tend to agree with the political positions taken by that particular party. If they vote at all, they tend to vote for that party's candidates.

In one sense, then, being a Democrat or a Republican means simply saying you are one. It means declaring that you sympathize with the beliefs and goals of that party.

In some cases, however, it means formally identifying yourself with the party. Some states ask voters to register by party. All voters have to declare themselves to be either members of a particular party or to be independents. In those states that hold closed primaries, only people registered as members of a party can vote in that party's primary elections.

People who want to become full-fledged active members of a major party can join at the local, state, or national level—or at all three at once. The procedure is usually very simple. In most places, it amounts to filling out a short form and paying dues.

In the state of Wisconsin, for instance, there are no age or residency qualifications for membership in the state Democratic party. Dues are fourteen dollars a year for most adults, and only seven dollars for what the party calls "seniors." Similarly, there are no qualifications for belonging to the Wisconsin Republican party.

Unless you actually want to participate in party business, there is little reason to go that far. Even people who are not official party members often can attend local party meetings and take part in discussions. Usually, only actual party members are eligible to vote in party caucuses, however, or to become delegates to party conventions.

Teenagers and those in their twenties who want to become more active in party political affairs can also join groups like the Young Republicans or the Young Democrats.

▶ Where Do the Parties Get Their Support?

Each of the two main parties claims to represent the best interests of all Americans. Nonetheless, neither party has won the allegiance of the majority of

American voters. According to the 1991 Gallup Organization Poll, 40 percent of voters say they are Democrats, while 32 percent say they are Republicans. The rest call themselves independents, or identify with a third party.[1]

In general, the Republican party is supported by big business, as well as by small businesspeople and by wealthy individuals who see it as the party of lower taxes and less government interference with business. It also has the support of many middle-class social conservatives and Christian fundamentalists, who see it as the party that most shares their values.

The Democratic party, on the other hand, is heavily supported by large labor unions, who see it as a defender of the rights of working men and women. It is also supported by many, especially feminists and civil rights advocates, who favor equal rights and opportunities for all people.

These are generalizations. Not all businesspeople are Republicans, and not all labor leaders are Democrats. Not all Christian fundamentalists are Republicans, either. These generalizations reflect the way most Americans view the parties and what they expect from them.

To some extent, the Republican party is still seen as the party of the wealthy, the privileged, and the conservative. The Democratic party is still seen as the party of minorities, unionized workers, and the poor. The loyalties of the middle class are divided between the parties.

Roughly the same percentage of white Americans identify with each major party. The big difference comes among minorities, nearly 68 percent of whom are Democrats, but only 12 percent Republicans.

Divided by income classes, the Democrats' highest percentage of supporters (48 percent) is among those who make under $15,000 a year. The percentage of Republican supporters goes up steadily as the voters' incomes go up.

Among major religious groups, Baptists and Catholics are the most heavily Democratic, while Presbyterians, Mormons, and Episcopalians are the most heavily Republican.

The most Republican region of the country is the West, where about 36 percent of the people support that party. The most Democratic region is the East, where 44 percent of the people consider themselves Democrats, followed by what remains of the once solid South.

▶ Republican Factions

Today's major parties might sympathize with George Washington's warning against factions. Each of them is torn by factions of its own.

Each party is actually many different parties. At the top is a Democratic or Republican National Committee, made up of powerful party figures from around the country, and headed by a chairperson chosen by the committee. These committees are in charge of the day-to-day activities and overall strategy of the national party. When a party has a President in the White House, however, the

President is considered the head of the party and usually handpicks the chairperson of the National Committee.

Aside from each of these national bodies, however, there are hundreds of local and state party organizations. Most counties in every state have their own Republican and Democratic party organizations. Highly populated counties have several of them.

This might seem more highly organized than it really is. These organizations are actually very independent from each other. There is really no one in charge of the local organizations as a whole. The local organizations do not report to, or take instruction from, the national party. In some states, the local and state organizations are so separated that local party leaders do not even know who in their own community belongs to the state party.[2]

County and state party groups sometimes take very different stands from each other, and from the national party. Republican party organizations in parts of California, for example, are much more conservative than those in other parts of the state, but much less than those in a more liberal state like New York.

In the 1950s and 1960s, the national Republican party was torn by conflict between its "liberal" wing, led by Governor Nelson Rockefeller of New York, and its conservative wing, led by Senator Barry Goldwater of Arizona. More moderate Republicans, who wanted to find what they saw as more practical approaches to the nation's problems, were caught in the middle.

The conservatives took over the party in 1964 and nominated Goldwater for President. When Goldwater lost in a landslide, the more moderate Republicans took over the party, nominating Richard Nixon at the next convention.

The pragmatic moderates were less ideological than either the Goldwater or Rockefeller forces. They believed that compromise between the more extreme wings of the party was the only way for the Republicans ever to become a majority party. It seemed to work, at least for a while. Nixon was elected to two terms as President, and was succeeded by his even more moderate Vice President, Gerald Ford. Nixon picked Ford at least partly because he was so moderate that he would be a noncontroversial choice.

The conservatives never gave up. They kept working at the grassroots level, gaining control of many local Republican branches. When Ford lost the 1976 election to a Democrat, Jimmy Carter, the conservatives were ready. They took control of the party again at the 1980 convention, and for President nominated Ronald Reagan, who had become their hero as governor of California and spokesperson for the conservative cause.

By that time, voters were disillusioned with President Carter because of inflation at home and trouble in Iran. The Republicans swept in with an easy victory.

In the Congressional elections of 1994, Republicans took control of both the Senate and the House of Representatives for the first time in nearly half a century. The conservative wing is still in control of the party. The liberal wing has all but disappeared, but there are still factions among the Republicans, including many moderates, as well as many Christian fundamentalist Republicans who want the party to take even more conservative social positions than before.

▶ Democratic Factions

The divisions among the Republicans are nothing compared to those among Democrats. The Democratic party traditionally has been a "bigger tent" than their rivals. That is, it has had a wider variety of groups and interests within it. The party's inside quarrels are so many that they've become almost a matter of pride. Democrats are fond of quoting a crack made by the humorist Will Rogers: "I do not belong to any organized political party. I'm a Democrat."

In 1968, the party split so badly over the Vietnam War that the antiwar liberal Eugene McCarthy campaigned for the party's presidential nomination against the sitting President, Lyndon Johnson. Johnson decided not to run again. Meanwhile, George Wallace, the Democratic governor of Alabama, was so upset with Johnson's support of African-American civil rights that he launched a third-party candidacy. Almost 10 million people voted for him, most of them probably Democrats.

Liberals took over the Democratic party in 1972 and nominated George McGovern for President. McGovern lost the election in a landslide. As a result of the liberal candidate's crushing defeat, moderate and even conservative Democrats have been gaining influence in the party ever since.

The popularity of Ronald Reagan's conservative administration pushed the Democrats toward the right in the 1980s. In 1992, Bill Clinton won the presidency as a "new kind of Democrat"; he was not as liberal on many social issues as Democratic nominees had been in the past. He supported the death penalty, for example, as well as a number of economic and political reforms, like the line item veto, that were championed by the conservatives.

Like President Clinton, the Democratic party today is much more moderate than it used to be. The liberal wing of the party still exists, however. It is represented in the Senate by the veteran Senator Edward Kennedy of Massachusetts and the newcomer Senator Paul Wellstone of Minnesota. In the House, it is represented by Representative David Obey of Wisconsin and the African-American representatives who call themselves the Congressional Black Caucus. Although they are less powerful than they were twenty years ago, liberals continue to press for more generous social welfare programs, and for stronger civil rights protections for minorities.

▶ The Value of Factions

Factionalism can do great damage to a political party. The split between Republican liberals and conservatives nearly destroyed the party in the early 1960s, for instance. Conservative Democrats—especially in the South—often bolt the party to vote for Republicans in presidential elections. Since 1980, when they deserted a Democratic President, Jimmy Carter, to vote for Ronald Reagan, a Republican, they have been called "Reagan Democrats."

Even so, some students of politics, like Assistant Professor Denise Baer of American University, believe that factionalism actually strengthens the parties. They argue that disagreements are bound to arise inside the party. Allowing groups to battle among themselves in party caucuses and conventions is a good way for party members to work out these conflicts.

The alternative is for the party to split apart into a variety of other, smaller parties. This could make them less effective in working for the goals and principles that most party members still have in common, despite their other differences.

"The agreement is to have the debates within the family," Baer explains.[3] Once the factions inside the party have reached compromises among themselves, they can unite to promote their joint interests in election campaigns or on the floor of Congress.

The Parties' Role in Government

Although the United States Constitution does not mention political parties, they play a key role in the American system of government. In fact, they play many roles.

▶ Choosing Candidates

The key to the importance of parties in the United States political system is the process by which candidates are nominated for political office. Most candidates for major offices run as the candidates of one major party or another. Most of the rest are nominated by third parties, or even by a third party along with one of the two major ones.

Almost every current governor, senator, or congressperson was nominated by one of the two major parties. In fact, under the United States system, the job of nominating serious candidates for important offices is left almost entirely to these two institutions.

It is possible for independent candidates who have not been nominated by any party to run for office, but it is extremely hard for them to get on a state or national ballot, and almost impossible for them to get elected. State laws require nonparty candidates to meet a variety of specific qualifications before their names can be put on the ballot.

The toughest requirement in many states is that a certain number of registered voters must sign petitions for each person who wants to run for office. The number of signatures needed is usually so high that it is hard for candidates without helpful party organizations to collect enough signatures.

▶ How the Parties Choose Their Candidates

Parties pick candidates in three main ways:

A primary is a kind of preelection election. The voters choose between the candidates who want a particular party's backing in the general election. The candidates campaign much as they would in a regular election. The winners of each party's primary then face off against each other in the general, final election that determines who will actually get the office.

Candidates for many federal as well as state offices are chosen in primaries. There are no national primaries, however. Even presidential primaries are state elections, in which the voters decide on the candidate that each state's delegates will support for President.

Ultimately, of course, the presidential candidate

of each party is formally picked at the party's national convention. Some state parties hold their own state conventions, where party business is done, positions on issues are discussed, and candidates for major state offices are chosen.

Other state parties choose candidates in caucuses. These are meetings of party members, often held at the local or county level. Caucuses are frequently held to pick candidates for relatively minor offices that are not considered important enough to be worth either the attention of a state convention or the expense of a primary election.

▶ Choosing Presidents

In essence, it is the major parties, even more than the voters or the electoral college, that choose our Presidents for us. No one who was not nominated by one of them has become President since the Republican party was founded.

Although the parties formally name their candidates at their national conventions, the real choice has usually been made long before the delegates arrive, because most of the delegates come already committed to vote for particular candidates.

There used to be more suspense at national conventions. The majority of convention delegates were picked by the state or national parties, and most individual delegates were free to vote for any candidate they chose. When they got together at the convention, they made deals. The party bosses traded favors in return for votes for particular candidates.

A nineteenth-century state party convention in Illinois. The women sat in the gallery.

In 1968, however, the Democratic party convention in Chicago nominated Hubert Humphrey for President. Humphrey was Lyndon Johnson's Vice President, and he had the support of most of the Democratic party leaders, but Humphrey had lost every primary election in which he ran.[1] He backed Johnson's war policies in Vietnam, but the majority of Democratic voters had voted for peace candidates like Eugene McCarthy or Robert Kennedy.

A lot of those voters were outraged by the convention's choice. They pressed for reforms that would bind delegates chosen in state primaries and caucuses to vote for specific candidates. This meant that the nominated candidate would be decided upon not by party leaders but by ordinary primary voters. The Republicans followed the Democrats' lead, as more and more state party organizations went to binding primaries and caucuses. The result was a more democratic nominating process.[2]

▶ Open Primaries

Some states have taken the move toward more democracy in the nominating process one step further. They have opened up their primaries and caucuses, allowing any state residents to take part, whether they belong to the party or not.

The national parties do not really like these so-called open primaries. Why, they ask, should people who do not belong to the party be able to vote to nominate the party's candidate? Why should Democrats be allowed to help decide whom the

Republicans should nominate, and vice versa? In a state with no exciting Republican race to vote in, enough Republicans might vote in the Democratic primary to force the Democrats to nominate a Republican!

Just as important to loyal party members, the open primary makes party membership, and even party identification, less important. After all, if anybody can help nominate the party's candidate, what's the point of joining the party? What about those party members who have worked loyally to promote the party's goals and principles, and want to make sure the nominee represents their beliefs? Is it fair for them to be outnumbered in the primary by voters who have no real interest in the party at all?

In 1984, the national Democratic party announced that it would not accept delegates chosen in Wisconsin's open primary. They would accept only delegates chosen by Democrats, and Democrats alone. For that year, Wisconsin Democrats were forced to pick their delegates in caucuses held around the state. The move toward greater democracy was unstoppable, however. By the next presidential election in 1988, the national party relented and allowed Wisconsin to go back to its open primary.

By 1992, one or more parties in thirty-three states were holding open primaries or caucuses.

▶ Elections

In order to accomplish their other goals, parties need to get their candidates elected. For party workers, nothing is more important than getting votes. A sign hanging in the office of the Republican National Committee during the 1992 campaign said it all: "Great idea," proclaimed the sign, but "does it get us any votes?" If not, the sign implied, forget it.

The national parties raise lots of money and distribute it all around the country to party organizations that in turn spend most of the money promoting the campaigns of party candidates in state and national elections. This party money is often crucial to those campaigns.

The parties have a great advantage in raising money for candidates' campaigns, because there are legal limits on the amount of money any one person or organization can contribute to an individual candidate. These limits are designed to keep rich individuals, big businesses, and labor unions from "buying" candidates by pouring overwhelming amounts of money into their campaigns. A candidate who receives a large sum of money from some person or interest group might feel obligated to that person or group.

The limits on campaign contributions do not apply to the parties. They are free to collect as much money as anyone wants to give, and to distribute it to any candidate they choose.

▶ The Parties in Congress

Party membership is very important in Congress. It even determines where representatives will sit. In both the House and the Senate, Democrats are seated on the left side of the chamber, and Republicans on the right.[3]

More importantly, the parties are vital to the way Congress is run. Much of the real work in both the House and the Senate is done in committees, which are made up of small numbers of congresspersons or senators. Every proposed bill is sent to one or more of these committees. The committee studies the bill, makes changes to it, and finally either sends it back to the whole Congress to be voted on, or kills it, so that it is never voted on at all. Unless a committee reports out the bill, it cannot be voted on by the entire House or Senate.

Membership on these powerful committees is determined by party membership. The majority of each committee belongs to the party that has a majority in that house of Congress. When the Republicans won control of both houses of Congress, in 1995, they won control of the committees as well. Since they have a majority in Congress, they get a majority of members of each committee. (The exceptions are the ethics committees, which have an equal number of members from each party to keep one party from using them to attack political opponents.) Committee members vote for the chairperson, so the chairperson is usually a member of the majority party as well.

The speaker of the House and the majority leader of the Senate are both chosen by the members of the majority party, as are other important officers. Members of the minority party select a minority leader in each house as well. Each party also has an officer called a whip in each house. The whips help to plan and carry out party strategy. They count probable votes on upcoming bills, and try to coax party members to vote with the party leadership on important issues.

In the tradition of the Democratic-Republicans, each party has its own caucus, made up of the party's members, in each house. They get together to discuss issues, and try to come up with compromises that the various factions within the party can support.

In theory, then, the majority party could control absolutely everything that goes on in Congress. It could make any rules it wanted, and pass any bills. In reality, things do not work that way, because there is no party discipline in Congress, the way there is in parliamentary countries like Canada and Great Britain. In those countries, party members are often required to vote the way the party leadership decides. In the United States, however, individual Democrats and Republicans are free to vote any way they choose.

Because of the factions within each party, votes in Congress rarely split along strict party lines. Some moderate Republicans frequently vote with the Democrats, while many conservative Democrats frequently vote with the Republicans.

Geography sometimes plays a part as well. Senators and representatives often vote according to the interests of their region rather than the desires of their party. Democrats, for example, have generally led the way in passing laws to limit tobacco use, and to warn people about the dangers of smoking. The Republicans have been much more suspicious of government interference with what they call smokers' rights. On this issue, however, Democrats from tobacco-growing states like North Carolina and Kentucky usually vote with the Republicans against the Democratic measures that are intended to discourage the use of tobacco.

▶ Party Loyalty and the Loyal Opposition

Even though there is no party discipline in Congress, party loyalty has a great effect on what legislators do. Senators and representatives often vote in ways that help their party or hurt the opposition. Although virtually no member of Congress votes with his or her party on every vote, most of them vote with the party most of the time.

This is particularly true when it comes to close votes on measures proposed by the President. Members who belong to the same party as the President will sometimes vote for measures the President wants, even though they personally disagree with it. They do so because they do not want the President from their own party to lose on an important issue. In the same way, members of the opposition party sometimes vote against measures they do agree with, in order not to present a legislative victory to a President from the other party.

Some critics believe that this kind of party loyalty is a bad thing. They believe that legislators should always vote according to their own opinions, or else they should vote the way most of their constituents want them to vote. What their party wants should not matter.

Others insist that party loyalty is vital. They believe that it is only when party members work with each other, toward common goals, that the government can be run effectively.

Third Parties

Voters in the United States traditionally have split most of their votes between two political parties: first the Federalists and the Democratic-Republicans, and then the Democrats and the Whigs. Now, for almost a century and a half, votes have been split between the Republicans and the Democrats.

Americans have come to assume that there is something inevitable about this division into two parties, but there is nothing inevitable or magic about it. Nothing in the United States Constitution limits us to two political parties. In fact, nothing in the Constitution requires political parties at all.

Most modern democracies, in fact, have several active parties contesting for power. Canada and the United Kingdom, for example, usually have at least three or four parties represented in their legislatures. Other democratic legislatures are divided into so many competing parties that no single party can win, or keep, control of the government for long. They are usually governed by coalitions made up of members of several different parties, who agree to cooperate for a while in order to get something done.

So why do we always seem to divide into two main parties, when other democracies do not?

▶ Why Two Parties?

One reason is tradition. As Fred R. Harris of the University of New Mexico has pointed out: "In part . . . our two party system endures because it has always been that way."[1] There is more to it than that; laws in many states make it hard for third parties to get on the ballot.

Even more fundamentally, we have a winner-take-all method of choosing our leaders. We have one President, and no matter how many candidates run for the office, only one can win. What's more, each seat in the United States Senate and Congress is also contested individually. Once again, only one candidate, from one party, can win.

Some of the countries that have several major parties do things differently. They have proportional representation, which means that the party that gets the most votes gets the most seats in the legislature, the party that comes in second gets the second most representatives, the party that comes in third gets the third most, and so on. In the United States, no offices are given to anyone for coming in second, much less to anyone with fewer votes than that.

In theory, proportional representation could leave almost half the voters with no representation at all. Suppose the country were almost equally divided between Democrats and Republicans, with the tiniest majority being Democrats. The Democrats might well win every election for every office by a handful of votes. They would then have total control of the government, and the Republicans would have no representatives at all, despite the fact that there were almost as many of them.

It is not likely that one party would win every close two-way election, of course. What if there were three or more major parties involved? Suppose the country were divided among Republicans, Democrats, and some third party, with the Republicans getting about 40 percent of the vote, and each of the others about 30 percent each? The Republicans would easily win every three-way election. They would control every political office in the country, despite the fact that almost six out of every ten people had voted for someone else.

It may be fear of this kind of minority control of government that makes most voters stick with one of the two main parties.

▶ The Need for Third Parties

Although most Americans seem satisfied with having just two main parties, other Americans are not. These are the people who feel that neither the

Democrats nor the Republicans truly represent their views and interests.

As we have seen, the two main parties are actually quite close together on many issues. They tend to agree most often on the most important issues such as the United States system of government, capitalism, the need for a strong military, and so on. The two parties would argue that this is the way it should be. These are things that the overwhelming majority of Americans agree about as well. It is only right that the mainstream parties should share these fundamental beliefs.

What about those Americans who do not agree? What about those who believe in socialism, for example, or who desire a parliamentary form of government? What about those who want the United States to get rid of all its nuclear weapons? Or those who want to abolish taxes? Or those who disagree in any other fundamental way with both major parties? Where do they go to find a group that will represent their views?

The answer, traditionally, has been that they go to a third party.

▶ What Is a Third Party?

A third party is any party other than the big two. The term is misleading, because there can be more than one third party. In the election of 1980, for example, at least eleven third-party or independent presidential candidates were on ballots in more than one state.[2] There were others who were on only one ballot, or who campaigned for write-in votes.

Third parties form for various reasons. Some spring up to support the candidacies of specific individuals. The Bull Moose Party, for example, was a vehicle for Theodore Roosevelt to campaign for President in 1912. George Wallace established the American Independent Party when he lost his bid for the Democratic presidential nomination in 1968.

Other third parties, like the Socialist party, form around a political ideology. Still others arise to support a particular proposal or reform. The Greenback Party campaigned to take the United States' currency off the gold standard, for example. The Prohibition Party wanted to outlaw alcohol.

Ideological third parties often last a long time, although they rarely get more than a handful of votes in any election. Those parties that form around individual candidates, on the other hand, tend to disappear very quickly. Those that press for particular reforms often disappear when one of the major parties takes up their cause.

▶ Third Parties in Elections

Third parties have sometimes played important roles in United States history. The very first third party, the Anti-Masonic Party, held the first presidential nominating convention, in Harrisburg, Pennsylvania, in 1831.[3]

Some third parties have even had notable success in national elections. In the late nineteenth century, for example, the Greenback Party got almost a million votes and won fourteen seats in the House of Representatives. In the election of 1912, the

Socialist party won at least twelve hundred state and local offices across the country.[4]

In the presidential election of 1948, the candidates of the Progressive and the States' Rights Democratic parties each got more than a million votes. In 1968, George Wallace polled almost 10 million votes at the head of his own American Independent party.

Of course, the most successful third party of all has been the Republican party. It was the first third party—and so far the only one—actually to elect a President of the United States.

While no other third party has won the presidency, some have helped to determine who did. Running as the candidate of the Progressive, or "Bull Moose," party in 1912, Theodore Roosevelt actually came in second, ahead of the Republican candidate, William Howard Taft. Roosevelt, who had previously been a Republican himself, took more than enough votes from Taft to assure that the Democrat, Woodrow Wilson, would win.

In 1992, a Texas tycoon, H. Ross Perot, ran for President as an independent and won nearly 20 million votes. Although Perot denied that it was a political party, he had the support of an organization he called United We Stand America. Perot came in third, but he got enough votes to keep the winner, Democrat Bill Clinton, from getting a majority of the votes cast.

Third parties do not always affect elections in the way they would like. Henry Clay, a Whig, might have won the election of 1844 if the abolitionist Liberty party had not won just enough antislavery votes to throw New York's electoral votes to someone else. Those votes probably would have gone to Clay. Because they did not, James Polk, a southern Democrat who supported the expansion of slavery, slipped into office.

Most third-party presidential candidates know that they cannot win. The major parties are too powerful for that. Third-party candidates run as protest candidates, to offer those voters who are upset with both major parties a chance to register their anger.

▶ New Ideas

The most important role third parties play has nothing to do with elections, but with ideas. Third parties historically have been a rich source of political ideas and a great spur to reforms.

Many of today's most popular government programs and policies began as proposals of one third party or another. Two third parties, the Liberty party and the Free Soil party, first made the abolition of slavery a major political issue in the 1840s, for example. The Populist party called for a national income tax, a secret ballot, and the direct election of United States senators long before these things became reality. The Socialist party, among others, pressed for many of the measures that are part of today's Social Security system.

What usually happens is that a third party raises an issue and presses for a new program or reform. At first, both major parties resist the idea. Once the

Jeremiah Simpson, a Populist party orator "on the stump" in rural Kansas. The Populists were an important third party in the Midwest.

third party makes a strong enough case to attract many voters to its position, however, one of the two main parties takes up the idea. The Republicans, for example, took the idea of a national income tax from the Populists.

▶ Third Parties Today

Although many Americans are unaware of them, there are many third parties in the United States today. Among the most significant are the Libertarian party, which works to end what it sees as the government's interference in individuals' private lives; the Right to Life party, which fights against legal approval of abortion; and a variety of left-wing and right-wing parties, each of which works to promote its own radical ideology.

Most of these third parties are very small. Some, like the Liberal party and the Socialist Workers' party, have been around for many decades. Others appear and disappear almost overnight.

It is unlikely that any of today's third parties will blossom into major parties. It is just as unlikely that any new major party will spring up anytime soon. The Republicans and the Democrats seem too firmly entrenched for that. However, today's third parties still have vital roles to play in American political life.

Third parties offer a refuge to people whose opinions are out of the political mainstream. They serve as platforms from which protest candidates can challenge the policies of those in power. They introduce new ideas to fuel the American political debate and keep it lively.

Republican sergeants-at-arms took up their rifles to drive out members of the Populist party, who had occupied the Kansas state house in 1893.

New third parties may yet come along that will sweep away today's major parties as swiftly and completely as the Republicans once swept away the Whigs.

Two hundred years have passed since George Washington warned the nation against the dangers of factions. During that time, it has become clear that factions—political parties—are inevitable in any active democracy.

More than being just inevitable, it seems that they are necessary.

Those countries that forbid political parties, or limit politics to one state-approved party, are not real democracies at all. In theory, political differences can be debated and worked out without the help of party organizations. In reality, people will always band together to work for common goals.

Political disputes can be settled within a single party, too. When there is no possible alternative for those who lose such battles, the single party becomes the real power in the country, more important even than the government itself. Since the party claims to stand for certain ideals, people who do not share its goals are forbidden to join. Everyone who does not belong is shut out of the political process. As a result, there is no real competition between ideologies and interests, and no real democracy.

Those countries that are really serious about democracy, on the other hand, encourage the formation of political parties, and they encourage those parties to compete in open and free elections.

George Washington was right about many things, but history has proven that he was wrong about political parties. Far from destroying democracy, strong and vigorous political parties are essential to the health of any democratic government.

Glossary

act—A bill, both before and after it has become law; such as the Civil Rights Act of 1964.

bill—A proposed law submitted to a legislative body.

boss—An old-time local political leader.

caucus—1. A group within a larger group that meets to discuss common interests or to plan strategies for action. 2. Any private meeting of such a group. 3. A meeting of party members specifically to nominate candidates for office.

closed primary—A primary election in which only registered members of a particular political party can vote. See also **primary** and **open primary**.

Cold War—A nonmilitary struggle between potential military enemies. Specifically, the conflict from 1945 to 1989 between the Western nations and the Communist bloc led by the Soviet Union.

conservative—As opposed to **liberal**. 1. Refers to the beliefs of those who tend to oppose governmental efforts to interfere with the economic affairs of individuals and businesses, and to favor governmental support for traditional moral values. In general, the Republican party is considered more conservative than the Democratic party. 2. Someone who holds such beliefs.

constituency—The people represented by an officeholder or political party.

democracy—A system of government in which final authority rests with the people. The United States is a representative democracy, in which the citizens elect individuals to represent them in the government.

election—A process by which the people cast votes to choose who will serve in public office.

electoral college—A system established by the Constitution to determine the winner in presidential elections according to the votes cast within each state. The number of electors is equal to the total number of the state's representatives in the House and Senate. Each elector casts one vote for the candidate who has won the most popular votes in the state. In order to be elected, a candidate must get a majority of the votes in the electoral college.

faction—A small group within a party that works together against another group, or groups, within the same party.

ideology—A combination of ideas and values.

independent—A voter, candidate, or officeholder who is not a member of any political party.

interest group—An organization of people who share certain concerns or interests, and who join together to influence governmental actions in regard to these interests. In a sense, a political party can be considered either a very broad interest group, or a collection of interest groups.

kickback—An illegal payment given to an officeholder as a reward for a share in the business done with the government.

laissez-faire—A policy that keeps government out of business affairs.

left—Toward the more liberal side of an issue, or of the political spectrum as a whole. See also **right**.

liberal—As opposed to **conservative**. 1. Refers to the beliefs of those who tend to favor the social welfare and regulatory functions of the federal government, and to oppose governmental efforts to interfere with the moral choices of individuals. In general, the Democratic party is considered more liberal than the Republican party. 2. Someone who holds such beliefs.

Glossary

line item veto—A proposal that would give the President the power to veto specific provisions of a bill, rather than the whole bill. It would allow Presidents to reduce government spending by eliminating individual programs.

major party—The Democratic or Republican party.

minor party—Any political party other than the Democratic or Republican party.

nominate—1. To propose someone for a position. 2. To choose a candidate for election to office. Parties nominate candidates.

nominee—A person who has been chosen as a candidate by a political party. Bill Clinton was the Democratic party's nominee for President in 1992.

open primary—A primary election in which voters can participate in choosing the nominees of a political party without registering as members of that party; as opposed to a closed primary. See also **primary** and **closed primary**.

partisan—Having to do with a party or faction. "Partisan activity" refers to actions taken on behalf of, or in support of, a particular party or cause.

patronage—The awarding of government jobs to political supporters and friends.

platform—A document put out by a political party, stating its principles and/or positions (planks) on specific issues.

political—Having to do with the activities of government in general, or partisan politics in particular.

political machine—A powerful local, county, or state political organization.

politics—1. The art or science of government. 2. The work of politicians. Often used as an insult, implying a lack of real principles, as in "That person is just playing politics."

primary or **primary election**—A preliminary election in which candidates are chosen to run in the final election which actually will determine who wins the office. See also **closed primary** and **open primary**.

proportional representation—A political system in which the party that gets the most votes gets the most legislative seats.

right—Toward the more conservative side of an issue, or of the political spectrum as a whole. See also **left**.

run—To campaign for public office.

tariff—A tax on foreign goods.

third party—Any political party other than the Democratic or Republican party. See also **minor party**.

Chapter Notes

Chapter 1

1. *Congressional Quarterly Guide to U.S. Elections,* 3rd edition (Washington, D.C.: Congressional Quarterly, 1994), p. 179.

Chapter 2

1. *Shorter Oxford English Dictionary,* 3rd edition (London: Oxford, 1969), vol. 2, p. 1537.

Chapter 3

1. "George Washington's Farewell Address—1796," reprinted in *By These Words, Great Documents of American Liberty, Selected and Placed in Their Contemporary Settings,* by Paul M. Angle (New York: Rand McNally, 1954), p. 141.

2. Ibid.

Chapter 4

1. Eric Foner and John A. Garraty, eds., "Corrupt Bargain," in *The Reader's Companion to American History,* (Boston: Houghton Mifflin, 1991), p. 236.

2. The description of Mrs. Samuel H. Smith quoted in *American History: A Survey,* 4th edition, Richard N. Current, T. Harry Williams, and Frank Freidel, eds. (New York: Knopf, 1975), p. 261.

3. Ibid.

4. Eric Foner and John A. Garraty, eds., "Spoils System," in *The Reader's Companion to American History* (Boston: Houghton Mifflin, 1991), p. 1021.

Chapter 6

1. Michael Kronenwetter, *The Threat From Within: Unethical Politics and Politicians* (New York: Franklin Watts, 1986), p. 48.

2. Eric Foner and John A. Garraty, eds., "Urban Bosses and Machine Politics, in *"The Reader's Companion to American History* (Boston: Houghton Mifflin, 1991), p. 1099.

Chapter 7

1. Quoted in Richard N. Curmont, et al, *American History* (New York: Knopf, 1975), pp. 582–583.

2. "Vietnam: 'We Seek No Wider War,'" *Newsweek,* August 17, 1964, p. 17.

3. "Chronology: Generation of Conflict," *Time,* November 6, 1972, pp. 28–29.

Chapter 8

1. This and other quotes explaining Republican beliefs in this section are from *The Republican Platform 1992,* adopted August 17, 1992, and available from the Republican party, Washington, D.C.

2. *The Democratic Party Platform 1992,* adopted at the 1992 Democratic National Convention, and available from the Democratic National Committee, Washington, D.C.

Chapter 9

1. The statistics in this section come from *The World Almanac of U.S. Politics* (New York: World Almanac, 1991), p. 25.

2. Interview with Marathon county, Wis., Republican party chairman Dave Torkko, May 24, 1994.

3. Speech by Denise Baer given at the Lobbying Institute Conference, American University, Washington, D.C., December 29, 1993.

Chapter 10

1. *1992 Race to the Nomination: A State by State Guide to the Nominating Process* (Washington, D.C.: Congressional Quarterly, undated), p. 2.

2. William Crotty, *Decision for the Democrats* (Baltimore: Johns Hopkins University Press, 1978), p. 72.

3. Fred R. Harris, *America's Democracy: The Ideal and the Reality* (Glenview, Ill.: Scott Foresman and Company, 1980), p. 391.

Chapter 11

1. Fred R. Harris, *America's Democracy: The Ideal and the Reality* (Glenview, Ill.: Scott Foresman and Company, 1980), p. 250.

2. *The World Almanac of U.S. Politics* (New York: World Almanac, 1991), p. 23.

3. Richard N. Curront, et al., *American History* (New York: Knopf, 1975), p. 261.

4. Eric Foner and John A. Garraty, eds., *The Reader's Companion to American History* (Boston: Houghton Mifflin, 1991), p. 1002.

Further Reading

Bernhard, Winfred E., Felice A. Bonadio, and Morton Borden, eds. *Political Parties in American History*. New York: G. P. Putnam's Sons, 1974.

Binkley, Wilfrede E. *American Political Parties: Their Natural History*. New York: Alfred A. Knopf, 1964.

Burdett, Franklin, *The Republican Party*. New York: Van Nostrand, 1972.

Chambers, William Nesbit, and Walter Dean Burnham. *The American Party System*. 3rd edition. New York: Oxford University Press, 1975.

Crotty, William J. *Decision for the Democrats: Reforming the Party Structure*. Baltimore: Johns Hopkins University Press, 1978.

Harris, Fred R. *America's Democracy: The Ideal and the Reality*. Glenview, Ill.: Scott Foresman and Company, 1980.

Hesseltine, William B. *Third-Party Movements in the United States*. New York: Van Nostrand, 1962.

Kent, Frank R. *Democratic Party: A History*. New York: Johnson Reprint, 1968.

Kronenwetter, Michael. *The Threat From Within*. New York: Franklin Watts, 1986.

Lowe, Carl, ed. *New Alignments in American Politics*. New York: H. W. Wilson, 1980.

1992 Race to the Nomination: A State by State Guide to the Nominating Process. Washington, D.C.: Congressional Quarterly, undated.

Rossiter, Clinton. *Parties and Politics in America*. Ithaca, N.Y.: Cornell University Press, 1960.

Sorauf, Frank J. *Party Politics in America*. New York: Little Brown, 1976.

The World Almanac of U.S. Politics. New York: World Almanac, 1991.

Index

Index

Harris, Fred R., 106
Harrison, Benjamin, 54
Harrison, William Henry, 35
Hatfield, Mark, 82
Hayes, Rutherford B., 46
Humphrey, Hubert, 66, 98

J
Jackson, Andrew, 28, 29,
    31-32, 34, 35, 59, 61
Jackson, Jesse, 8
Jefferson, Thomas, 20, 25, 26,
    27, 29, 31,
Jeffersonians. *See*
    Democratic-Republican
    party.
Jeffersonian Republicans. *See*
    Democratic-Republican
    party.
Johnson, Andrew, 38
Johnson, Lyndon, 54, 62, 65,
    66, 68, 83, 91, 98
Jordan, Barbara, 7

K
Kansas-Nebraska Act, 37
Kennedy, Edward, 92
Kennedy, John F., 54, 58, 65,
    68, 82
Kennedy, Robert, 98
Ku Klux Klan, 46

L
laissez-faire, 60-61
Liberal party, 113
Liberty party, 111
Lincoln, Abraham, 38, 67, 75
Lyon, Matthew, 24

M
machines, political, 48-58
Madison, James, 20, 27
Mafia, 56
Marcy, William L., 32
McCarthy, Eugene, 91, 98

military spending, 62, 63, 65,
    80, 83
Miller, Zell, 7
money-raising, 100
Monroe, James, 27, 28

N
National Education
    Association, 77
New Deal, 61
Nixon, Richard, 66, 70, 71, 90
nuclear weapons, 83

O
Obey, David, 92

P
party. *See* political party.
party conventions, 5-10, 58,
    72-73, 86, 90, 93, 94-96,
    98
party loyalty, 103-104
party machines. *See* machines.
"party of the rich," 81
party organizations, state and
    local, 89
party platforms. *See* platforms.
party primaries. *See* primary,
    party.
Pendergast, Tom, 54
Perot, H. Ross, 110
Pierce, Franklin, 7
platforms, 6, 8, 72-73, 74, 77,
    78, 79, 83
political party, 12-14
    function of, 14
politics, definition of, 11
Polk, James, 111
Populist party, 111
primary, open, 98-99
primary, party, 56, 86, 95
Progressive party, 110
Prohibition, 55
Prohibition party, 109